SIX SECRETS MEN KEEP FROM WOMEN

1. Men may say that they want "Womanlove," but what they really seek from women is "Motherlove."

2. Men both want and fear being taken care of by women. They have a hidden desire to be fussed over by a woman—and then panic if they begin to feel trapped.

3. Men hide their desire for romance. The politics of being a man calls for men to play down their natural romanticism and sensuality.

4. Men grow secretly resentful of the roles they play with women, and they often become disenchanted with the role of family provider.

5. Sometimes men do not want sex. When men allow sexual prowess and performance to become a measure of masculinity, they defeat their own purpose by acting as if they want sex all the time.

6. Men sometimes fake orgasm. They decide they are better off faking one than having to deal with a wounded ego.

THE SECRETS MEN KEEP

Dr. Ken Druck

with James C. Simmons

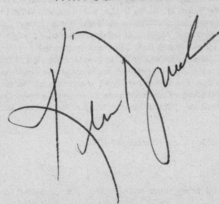

BALLANTINE BOOKS • NEW YORK

Grateful acknowledgment is given to the following for permission to reprint previously published material: Excerpt from *Sorties: Journals and New Essays* by James Dickey. Copyright © 1971 by James Dickey. Reprinted by permission of Doubleday & Company, Inc. Excerpt from *My Father, My Son* by Dr. Lee Salk. Copyright © 1982 by Dr. Lee Salk. Reprinted by permission of Putnam Publishing Group. Excerpt from *Men: A Book for Women* by James Wagenvoord and Peyton Bailey. Copyright © 1978 by James Wagenvoord and Peyton Bailey. Reprinted by permission of Avon Books, Inc. Excerpt from "Jake: A Man's Opinion," in *Glamour*. Copyright © 1980 by The Conde Nast Publications, Inc. Reprinted by permission of The Conde Nast Publications, Inc. Excerpt from *The Memoirs of Sherwood Anderson* by Sherwood Anderson. Copyright © 1942 Eleanor Copenhaver Anderson; copyright renewed 1969 by Eleanor Copenhaver Anderson. Reprinted by permission of Harold Ober Associates, Inc.

Library of Congress Catalog Card Number: 85-6744

ISBN 0-345-34132-5

This edition published by arrangement with Doubleday & Company, Inc.

Manufactured in the United States of America

First Ballantine Books Edition: June 1987

I dedicate this book to
Roslyn and Charles, my parents,
with the highest form of
gratitude I know,
my love.

K.D.

Acknowledgments

Nobody can imagine what it was like to live with me this past year and a half but my family. I must begin by acknowledging my life partner, Karen Druck, whose loving support was matched only by her rich contributions and incisive editorial input, and my dear children, Jenna and Stefie, whose love, hugs, and future were the sweetest incentives for completing this book.

I wish to thank my dear friend Jim Sanderson, syndicated columnist and prolific writer on men's issues, who contributed generously to this book. With the utmost love and appreciation one man can have for another, I wish to recognize my late friend, Terry Koppenhaver, who died shortly before publication. Terry was the kind of friend who comes but once in a lifetime.

And to those whose contributions to my life and work I will always remember: Harold and Sirah Bloomfield, Norman Cousins, Israel Druck, Paul Druck, Joseph Ducoff,

Godfred Germansky, Mark Gerzon, Ruth and Manny Gold-stein, Bonnie and Jim Hall, James Harrison, Richard Hyc-ner, Ellen McCoy, Joan and Bill Nemour, Al Pesso, Roberta and Joe Pirrello, Anne Schaef, the Schuster clan, and my colleagues at the Fielding Institute.

Special thanks to:

Howard Morhaim, our agent, who turned out to be the effective and sensitive man this book aspires to help men become.

Adrian Zackheim, our editor, and the entire Doubleday team.

The members of the San Diego Author's Group, espe-cially Margaret McBride, who introduced me to James Sim-mons, my collaborator on this book.

James Simmons wishes to thank in particular Karma Still and Deborah Ariely, who patiently read through the various drafts of this book and offered up thoughtful criticism.

Lastly, I wish to thank the men in the Alive and Male seminars and support groups (and their families) and my clients in private practice in San Diego for allowing me to be a part of and learn from their lives.

KEN DRUCK, PH.D.

Contents

The Secrets Men Keep

Men today are the guardians of some of the world's best-kept secrets. We lead secret emotional lives, often hiding our deepest fears and insecurities, as well as our most cherished dreams, even from those we love and trust. Perhaps we are hiding a fear we have carried around our entire life, perhaps a secret fantasy. Or we may be more sensitive and, as a consequence, more easily hurt than we care to admit.

We block off entire areas of ourselves, stamp them "TOP SECRET," and file them away. And we keep their very existence a secret from wives, girlfriends, children and buddies. We see these parts of whom we are as a threat. Perhaps they embarrass us. Or maybe they fail to confirm a particular image we have set out to project for others.

We select any number of places in which to hide our secrets. We disguise them in roles like "Mr. Nice Guy" or

"The Hard-driving Businessman." Our former jobs and failed marriages may have been burial grounds for secrets. Even our greatest successes can become hiding places for our deepest secrets.

But secrets have a way of making their presence felt. We may think that we are done with them, having filed them away and forgotten about them. But they are still there, often disguised in a stubborn feeling of unhappiness or uneasiness that refuses to go away. Perhaps they appear in a health crisis, such as an ulcer, high blood pressure, or a heart attack. Or they may come out in a sudden burst of temper, directed against our wives, kids, boss, or the world in general.

There is a distressing irony here. We live in the Age of Information, in which giant new computers process one billion bits of data almost instantaneously. We spend large amounts of time and energy assimilating new information. And yet at the same time we stubbornly avoid processing certain kinds of information about ourselves.

Many men end up prisoners in their jobs and relationships, held captive by their secrets. Stan, a client of mine, finally broke out of his secret hiding place and revitalized himself, as well as his marriage.

"My wife thought she knew everything there was to know about me. But there were a number of important things I had kept from her. Some of them I had trouble admitting to myself. Like how frustrated I felt about work. My father had been an unhappy man. I was becoming more like him every day. I can see now how my refusal to talk about these feelings with my wife affected our marriage. My secrets were like walls keeping us apart.

"After fourteen years on the same job, I hated what had become of my life. Like my father, I put in ten-hour workdays, six days a week. And like my father, I came home exhausted and kept to myself. I never felt I had the right to complain. My wife would ask if I was all right and I'd tell her, 'Leave me alone, I'm tired, that's all.' Inside, I was dying a little bit each day.

"Then my wife became ill. That changed everything. For the first time, I faced losing her. Both Lynn and I started opening up to one another. I told her how unhappy I'd been. I was surprised she had many of the same feelings. Listening to her, I felt relieved. We discussed ways that we could change our lives around. It was like lifting a tremendous burden off my shoulders. My unhappiness was no longer something I had to keep locked up inside.

"For the first time in years I did not feel alone. Lynn recovered and we were more like partners than ever before. I made some changes in my crazy work schedule. I'm a lot happier now. It took me a long time to accept how I really felt, and even longer to speak up. Saying what's really on my mind is still awkward, but that's all right. I'm doing a lot better."

Webster's Dictionary tells us that the word "secret" comes from the Latin *secretus*, meaning "to set apart." Forever hidden away, our secrets set us apart, keeping who we really are an enigma.

There is another irony here. Secrets are, by definition, meant to be kept. Yet it is their destiny to be told. Life itself is a secret unfolding. Nature (including human nature) provides endless mysteries, riddles, and camouflages, as well as endless discoveries. It is in the process of uncovering and telling our secrets that life takes on meaning. We learn to cultivate a relationship with the mysteries, as well as the realities, which confront us.

This book is an outgrowth of my work in the area of

male psychology over the past twelve years. In addition to my general practice, I have worked extensively with men, particularly in the context of the Alive and Male seminars that I have conducted across the United States. College professors and plumbers, judges and retired Army officers, doctors and business executives have come together in these seminars to acknowledge and understand their individual and collective secrets. They have broken what I call "the silent barrier." In the seminars, we discuss our relationships with our fathers, mothers, life partners, buddies, jobs, and children. By the end of each seminar, these men discover that the inner life of a carpenter is not that much different from that of a surgeon. We all share pretty much the same fears and hopes. My work with these men, the participants in my men's groups, and the men and women I see in my private practice in San Diego form the basis for this book. From all of them, I have learned that beyond secrecy lies the "real" strength and sensitivity every man wants in himself—and what every woman wants in a man.

THE RIGHT STUFF OR THE RIGHT BLUFF?

The central idea of this book is simple: To be truly successful and happy, men must learn to trade in their secrets for sincerity. Webster's Dictionary defines "sincerity" as "honesty of mind or intention; truthfulness; genuineness." To be sincere, we must first be ourselves. We cannot approach people in our lives as if they were opponents in a poker game where deception (or bluffing) is commonplace. Sooner or later, we must all lay our cards down on the table. When we make a sincere and honest disclosure of who we are, we cease being players in a staged game. We become instead full participants in the adventure of life.

THE MAJOR AREAS IN WHICH MEN KEEP SECRETS

Men secretly yearn for their father's love and approval.

A majority of men did not receive the love, approval, and direct contact they wanted from their fathers. Often they are unaware that "the search for father" is behind their drive to prove themselves over and over. Too many men perceive their yearning for their father's love as a sign of immaturity. "Men are supposed to stand on their own," they tell themselves. "We should outgrow our need for Father." But the truth, as revealed by the men themselves, is that many are still tied to their fathers for approval, whether those fathers are dead, live far away, or have become estranged.

Men hide their desire for friendship and support from other males.

Many men have stopped believing that close companionship is possible, except with women. They may have a buddy or two on the "inactive" list whom they call once every year or so. But few men have one close male friend in whom they can confide. They appear aloof and indifferent toward most male peers, pretending that such relationships are not important. Instead men choose to hide behind their job titles and the excuse that "I've outgrown my need for buddies." But they remember fondly the memories of the good times they shared in their youth with their close buddies. Men secretly miss the close companionship that those friendships in high school, college, and the armed services afforded them.

Men use the workplace as a major burial ground for
their secrets.

Our work can either be a source of enormous personal
fulfillment or a burial ground for some of our most disturbing fears and secrets. Work can be the stage on which
many of our greatest performances in life are given and our
most satisfying moments are lived. Men who love their
work are often sustained by it through losses, sudden
changes, or crises in other areas. Our jobs can challenge us
to use the fullest range of our talents and personalities by
helping us to achieve a level of excellence that we would
otherwise never have attained.

But there is also a danger here. Many men define themselves almost solely on the basis of what they do for a
living. They allow themselves to become overly dependent
on work to meet their personal needs, and lose part of their
humanity in the process. Perhaps the least acknowledged
and most secretive aspect of men's professional lives is
how much of a hiding place the workplace can be.

Men are much more dependent upon women than
they admit.

Men strive hard to present an image of themselves as
strong and independent. But women are not fooled. Wives,
lovers, and mothers have always known that even the most
powerful men are often dependent. Their mistake lies in
assuming that men themselves realize how dependent they
are upon women. But few do. Perhaps no secret is so hard
for men to confront as this one. Most men were raised by
their mothers and are still dependent upon them in ways
they never suspected. Until men resolve their feelings toward their mothers, it will be difficult for them to establish

and maintain a mature and satisfying relationship with another woman.

Men feel powerless and angry toward women.

Men's anger with women is another major secret, a genie that most men try to keep tightly bottled up. But it is only a matter of time before their anger is displaced as disinterest in romance and sex, quarreling, or constant busyness at the office. Most men were taught that love meant taking care of women, in return for the women taking care of their sexual, emotional, and custodial needs. This seems like a fine arrangement—until both men and women realize how powerless they have rendered themselves.

Men deny themselves the right to feel uncertain, fearful, and hurt.

This is the most central of men's secrets. Men experience a broad range of emotions, no matter how much they may deny it to others and themselves. Contrary to the reality that big boys *do* cry, men are taught from an early age that "big boys *don't* cry"—that is, it is *not* acceptable for men to show their emotions. Rather than risk demotion to the status of being "less than a man," men keep their emotions under cover. They have learned to master a host of disguises that allow them to pose as "unaffected." Men play it safe, figuring that others cannot hurt their feelings if they never show them those feelings.

THE BENEFITS OF ACKNOWLEDGING OUR SECRETS

This is a book about the power of disclosure. Disclosure is the least exploited form of power known to men. We are taught in every gesture to appear unaffected. We are trained to hide our emotions. We learn selective disclosure—the art of revealing only the most impressive parts of ourselves.

The process of confessing our secrets is often difficult and painful, which may explain why we live with them for so long. Yet the rewards men reap upon opening up their secret areas are many. Let's state a few of them:

Our whole world changes when we tell the truth.

Few experiences can be more liberating and cathartic than telling the truth about ourselves. Once we have done that, we have freed ourselves to set a new course for our relationships, rid ourselves of crippling burdens of guilt, and discovered new possibilities for us that we never before suspected. By telling a secret, we dispel destructive myths.

We fulfill our human need to be known and accepted.

By hiding our true selves and projecting false images in order to gain the approval of others, we never test our actual worth. Our images receive attention, but our inner selves never feel fully validated. By giving up our secrets, we may now gain real acceptance of ourselves from others.

We simplify our lives.

There are now no more excuses, lies, deceptions, or roles to play. We rid ourselves of all our fears about being found out. We free up the tremendous amounts of time and energy that normally go into maintaining secrecy.

We improve our relationships.

By doing away with secrecy, we eliminate all those discrepancies, inconsistencies, and confused messages that we had been sending out. We communicate loud and clear now: "What you see is what you get," and set the tone for a clearer understanding of one another.

We become more secure.

Without our secrets to weigh us down, we can allow our personality to unfold and ripen. We develop greater confidence, take more risks, and become more productive in our work because we are more self-assured.

WHAT IS A MAN TO BE?

All men are feeling the crunch on male identity from the social changes of the past fifteen years. We live in confusing and difficult times. Men today no longer know what it means to be a man. We are bombarded on every side by conflicting and contradictory signals from our wives, women friends, mothers, fathers, and peers. "Be strong but don't be macho," urges one voice. "Be sensitive but don't be a wimp," says another.

Today's men are uncertain about what they want and

what their choices are. Being a man in the eighties is hard
work if, as men, we take our signals from others.

WHAT WE WILL DO IN THIS BOOK

"Life is either a daring adventure or nothing at all,"
Helen Keller once said. We Americans have always been
adventurers. Our country's history has been one of succes-
sive waves of frontiers, on land, at sea, and now in space. I
think we are still explorers at heart. The age of discovery
may be over in the larger sense. But for the average person
it has hardly begun. Each of us carries a Lewis and Clark,
a Captain James Cook, or an Admiral Richard Byrd inside
us, just waiting to be set free.

The Secrets Men Keep offers the promise of a different
sort of exploration. "Be the Columbus to whole new conti-
nents and worlds within you, opening new channels, not of
trade, but of thought," the woodsman and philosopher
Henry David Thoreau urged almost 150 years ago. *The
Secrets Men Keep* is a navigational aid to exactly that sort
of exploratory journey.

This is a book about discovering new possibilities in
ourselves which we may never have believed existed. Each
of us shares a wellspring of hope about becoming all we
can be, of living out the best in us. But we need more than
hope. We need to take some risks, bet on ourselves, and
trust that there will be large payoffs in our lives.

The Secrets Men Keep offers no magical formula that
promises a new, trouble-free self within thirty days. But it
does recognize that we need to ask questions and to examine what is happening to men in a simple, straightforward
manner without imposing the additional burden of doc-
trine.

This is a book for men first. It deals directly with what it means to be a man in today's world through the accounts of men themselves. It provides the processes and imagery through which men can carve out their own alternatives to the old role models.

For those readers who wish to take a more active role in making certain key changes in their lives, I have included a series of exercises in each chapter. I have used these exercises successfully with men in seminars, workshops, and support groups across the United States. They are proven methods by which the reader can confront his fears and old images and move from secrecy toward openness. These exercises will allow the men reading this book to generate specific, personal data unique to their situations that will be enormously helpful to their understanding of their feelings on a broad range of personal issues.

I cannot urge too strongly that each reader buy a small notebook to use as a journal in which he can record his impressions and feelings while he does the exercises. When we articulate our feelings, thoughts, and experiences, we take a giant step toward understanding them. Not only will these written responses be a permanent record of where we came from but they will also let us know how far we have traveled.

WHO IS THE SUCCESSFUL MAN OF THE EIGHTIES?

This book provides the means for any man to become more successful and powerful by becoming more himself. Men must broaden their definition of success to include both the professional and personal spheres. To be a success in the eighties, men must learn to reach down inside themselves to make contact with what *they* feel, what *they* want, and what *they* believe it means to be a success. They must value self-disclosure and authenticity over secrecy. The successful man of today is one who has no patience with playing gender roles and would rather write his own ticket. He knows what he wants and feels, or he is actively trying to find out. He accepts those times when he feels uncertain, weak, or afraid—or when others do.

He is proud of his prowess at both sports and business. He thinks there is no reason why he should apologize for either his attractiveness to women or the money, power, and prestige he may have accumulated in his professional life. The successful man of the eighties does not wait for opportunities to develop. Rather he goes out and creates them. He knows that time and effort invested in his relationships, his profession, and his health today will repay him big dividends tomorrow.

Feelings: The Secret Garden Men Are Forbidden to Enter

ON BEING A MAN

"To be strong a man must be able to stand utterly alone, able to meet and deal with life relying solely upon his own inner resources," Watergate conspirator G. Gordon Liddy insisted. "Once I held my hand in the flame of a candle— just to see how tough I was."

No value has gotten modern American men into more trouble than that of "being a man." Traditional lore instructs us from a young age to "grow up and be a man." Not only is "be a man" as elusive and ambiguous a commandment as has ever been handed down, but we have no idea who originally gave it. Nor do we ever know exactly who is supposed to pass final judgment and tell us, "Good job! Now you're a MAN."

"Being a man" is male code for being "all grown up." "No more child in me," we declare from the podiums,

13

scaffolds, body-building studios, football fields, and office buildings. We were rushed to grow up and be "a man." All of a sudden a line was drawn. It was as if we heard our father's voice boom out, "It's time to grow up now. No more of this kid's stuff!"

One of my clients—let's call him Carl—can recall the exact moment when he made a psychological decision to grow up and "be a man." Carl was eight years old at the time. He made a feminine-like gesture with his hand. Suddenly, his father came over to him, squeezed his shoulder, and said roughly, "Don't be a sissy." Since that day Carl has secretly been ashamed of his hands and on guard against any gesture he might make which could be interpreted as feminine.

Most of us can remember some experience similar to Carl's. The admonitions still echo faintly in the caverns of our minds: "Don't be a mommy's boy!" "Don't cry!" "Take it like a man!" "Be a big boy now!" And then there came the time when we were embarrassed if our mother kissed or hugged us in front of our friends.

We got trapped at an early age in a set role. We were taught what is acceptable behavior for us, as little men, and what was unacceptable. We played hard at sports and fought for the right to be the King of the Mountain. We learned that such traits as toughness, rationality, aggression, competitiveness, self-reliance, and control over our emotions were positive for men, whereas tenderness, emotional sensitivity, dependence, openness to experience, and vulnerability were negative.

Most of us were raised thinking the American male had to be dominant. He does not crack, no matter what the stress. He is *always* a superb lover. We watched him parade before us on the movie screen in endless variations on the same theme: Humphrey Bogart, Gary Cooper, John Wayne, James Bond, Charles Bronson, Clint Eastwood. Always perfect. Always sure of himself. Always in control of the woman, the money, and the situation.

The trouble came when we tried to realize the image. And, of course, that was like wearing a suit two sizes too large. But we kept the suit in our closet anyway, right next to that plaque embossed with the "Commandments for Men" (courtesy of James Wagenvoord and Peyton Bailey's *Men: A Book for Women;* Avon Books, 1978):

Thou shall not cry.
Thou shall not display weakness.
Thou shall not need affection, gentleness, or warmth.
Thou shall comfort but not desire comforting.
Thou shall be needed but not need.
Thou shall touch but not be touched.
Thou shall be steel, not flesh
Thou shall be inviolate in your manhood.
Thou shall stand alone.

Here is an exercise that will allow you to begin taking a measure of where you stand on the important issue of what a man should be. What would your reactions be to the following situations? Would there be a discrepancy between your outward behavior as opposed to your inner feelings?

1. Your wife works. Would you feel comfortable helping with the housework, taking turns cooking dinner, and caring for the children?

2. You see two men walking down the street, their arms across one another's shoulders. Later a

male friend greets you with an unexpected hug. Are you comfortable with these signs of affection between men?

3. You have just lost your wife or girlfriend of five years' standing. She left you saying that she no longer loves you and wishes to start a new life. You, however, are still very much in love with her. Would you feel comfortable calling up a male friend and inviting him out, so that the two of you could discuss your problems and feelings?

4. It is your first date with a woman you have looked forward to seeing for several weeks. You approach the box office of the movie theater. As you reach for your wallet, your date says, "You drove. Why don't I buy the tickets?" Are you comfortable with that arrangement for the evening?

5. Later that same evening near the end of the movie, you suddenly find yourself deeply touched by what happens on the screen. Your throat tightens, and the tears well up in your eyes. Do you feel embarrassed, especially with your date sitting next to you, and choke back the emotions?

6. Several people have already been laid off in your office. Your boss has told you repeatedly that he thinks you are doing an excellent job. But you know that the company is going through some difficult times. Does the prospect of losing your job frighten you because you feel that without it you will lose much of your sense of self-worth?

7. You are in bed with a woman you have been seeing for several months. However, you are unable to keep an erection. Do you feel that your manhood has been compromised?

8. You are driving across town with your wife to a party. You get lost. Your wife suggests that you stop and ask for directions. Do you tell her, "Don't worry, dear, I'll get us there"—and then continue looking for the party until you find it?

9. You are at a picnic with some of your office mates and their families. Someone suggests a game of touch football. Eight of the men choose up sides and start to play. It has been a while since you have played and you are out of shape. Do you tell yourself not to worry and play hard so that your team will win?

10 You are on a visit to the Grand Canyon with your family, admiring the view from an over look. Suddenly, your daughter fumbles her Cabbage Patch doll and drops it over the edge. It lodges ten feet down in the rocks, a few feet from the edge of a much steeper drop. Your daughter sets up a howl. A sign on the railing warns: DANGER—DO NOT GO BEYOND THIS POINT. Do you climb down to retrieve the lost doll?

Notice how great or small the discrepancy is between what your outward and inner (secret) reaction would be in each of the above imagined situations. Try to measure to what extent your behavior would be determined by what you perceived your role as a man to be rather than by what you actually felt.

MEN AND THE MEGATRENDS

The fact is that numerous trends, already firmly entrenched in modern society, have eroded many of the traditional values by which men have taken their identity and exposed the traditional male hiding places. Men who insist upon clinging to the old definitions of what it takes to "be a man" will slowly find themselves marching along after the dinosaurs to an inglorious extinction. We live in a world completely different from the one in which our fathers were raised. If we rely simply upon the rules our fathers passed down to us, we will find ourselves woefully ill equipped to navigate the transitional years ahead.

The Vietnam veterans of the early seventies were perhaps the first men seriously affected by these changes. When they left for the war, it was fairly clear to most men that a man's job was to provide for his family and serve his country in time of need. The Vietnam veteran returned to the States a modern Rip Van Winkle to find himself in a vastly different world than the familiar one he remembered. One of my clients, Frank, a 35-year-old policeman, told me:

"When I got back from Nam, I had no idea I'd be treated like some baby killer, as if what happened over there was my fault. I went into the service because that was the thing to do. As a citizen of this country, I was supposed to defend our way of life. Sometimes I was afraid I'd come back to the States in a body bag, but I never expected to be treated like the bad guy."

Frank had found himself caught up in the early stages of a set of major trends—or megatrends, to use a currently fashionable word—that were radically altering American society and in particular the ways we view ourselves as men and women. For example, after the Second World War there was an emphasis upon symbols that polarized and exaggerated masculinity and femininity. Whether it was the big car or the buxom woman, male and female attributes were stereotyped exaggerations. Men who fit the mold of being tough and domineering were considered manly and thought to have fulfilled their adult roles as men. Women, in turn, put an emphasis on their appearance and placed their husbands and families first.

Then in the protest decade of the sixties these attitudes started to change. We had a rebellion against traditional values and the emergence of the women's movement with its concerns for sexual discrimination and inequality. The secret unhappiness of many women became widely publicized. Our world became increasingly more complicated. By the mid-seventies women began to enter the work force in unprecedented numbers. Lifestyles diversified. Inflation cast a cloud of uncertainty over the entire economy. We changed from an either/or world to one in which a multiplicity of choices is the norm.

Men who continued to measure their masculinity by their superior physical strength, athletic skills, martial arts, sexual prowess, and the size of their paychecks found themselves disoriented and threatened by a world in which women worked out with weights in body-building studios, raced down a basketball court, graduated from West Point, took the initiative in sex, and brought home a larger paycheck.

John Naisbitt's *Megatrends*, one of the best-selling books of 1983, defined some of the new directions radically transforming our lives at all levels. "We are living in the *time of parenthesis*, the time between eras," Naisbitt

observed. "It is as though we have bracketed off the
present from both the past and the future, for we are neither here nor there."

Let's examine briefly several additional trends that are
specifically impacting on men, particularly in the area of
the traditional views men have had of their "proper" roles:

- More and more American families are tossing tra-
  dition to the wind and putting wives—not husbands—in the role of the primary breadwinner.
  The 1980 census revealed that there are almost 6
  million families—12 percent of all U.S. couples
  —in which women earn more than their husbands.
  In 4 million of these families both the husband and
  the wife work. In 2 million only the wife is a wage
  earner. Thirty-six percent of the wives in these
  families hold professional or managerial positions.

- "Women have shown themselves to be very effective competitors with men for traditionally male
  jobs," says the head of the New York office of the
  Bureau of Labor Statistics. In the last decade,
  American women have moved steadily and inexo-
  rably into positions once considered the exclusive
  province of American men. For example, in the
  meat-packing industry automatic machines for
  moving sides of beef have eased the need for so
  much heaving and hoisting. Since 1970, the proportion of packinghouse butchers who are women
  has increased by more than one-third. Many of the
  major gains for women have been in the upper
  reaches of the workplace. From 1960 to 1983, the
  male proportion among lawyers dropped from 98

percent to 85 percent; in advertising, from 86 percent to 52 percent; and in banking and financial management, from 91 percent to 61 percent.

- Smokestack industrial America, where the work force is predominantly male, is undergoing major changes in order to become competitive once more in a world market. An army of robots, optical scanners, microchips, and other forms of sophisticated automation is revolutionizing the way companies produce and people work. But the cost in factory jobs in smokestack America will be enormous, as millions of mostly male workers in the steel, auto, textile, and other industries will see their jobs disappear. According to one report in *U.S. News & World Report*, over 30 million assembly-line workers in the next thirty years may lose their jobs to a new generation of intelligent robots.

- While men lose jobs, women gain disproportionately in those new ones created. The Labor Department projects that for the decade of 1985–95 two-thirds of all new jobs will go to women. "It is not that the new positions have a specific gender written on them," Andrew Hacker observed in the New York *Times*. "Despite recent changes stimulated by the women's movement, women in our society still tend to differ from men in upbringing and outlook, and some of their attributes have a tangible value in the current job market." For example, literacy with both words and numbers is a basic requirement for a broad range of jobs, from taking airline reservations to monitoring hospital intensive-care units. "For the first time in our history, women are clearly emerging as better educated than men," warns Hacker.

- The traditional two-parent family is fast giving way in the America of the 1980s to households in which one adult must juggle the often enormous demands of making a living and raising the children. Ten percent of these single-parent households are headed by men, and the number is growing rapidly each year. For many men the plight of Dustin Hoffman in the popular film *Kramer vs. Kramer* will be the reality in their future.

- The knowledge explosion affects directly men's influence as fathers. The growth of knowledge is now so rapid that even the most intelligent and intellectually oriented man cannot hope to stay abreast of all that is taught his children in school. And many fathers today are finding themselves increasingly on the wrong side of the computer-literacy gap. While they are secretly intimidated by and ignorant of computers, their children are computer whiz kids, developing a computer literacy in some cases as early as the second grade. Such developments obviously devalue the traditional role of the father as the fount of all knowledge and wisdom in the home.

Paul, 43, a freelance writer in the Seattle area, knows exactly how it feels to be positioned on the wrong side of one of these megatrends. Last year he earned $25,000. However, for the past three years his wife, Joyce, a woman twelve years his junior, has made $55,000 as a television news reporter and occasional anchorwoman. She is currently negotiating with one of the major networks for a move to New York City, which would double her salary. Paul was secretly troubled at times by the enormous discrepancy in their earning power until he finally spoke out to a friend.

"I know it's stupid of me but sometimes I feel resentful and a little frightened because Joyce is making so much more money than I do or ever will," Paul admitted candidly. "It really hurt when we bought our condominium two years ago, and Joyce fronted most of the down payment. Our savings are mostly *her* savings. I sometimes lie awake at night and worry about what it will be like with the two of us when she starts making a six-figure salary."

Paul's story suggests some of the emotional turmoil men secretly suffer when they are caught up in this tidal wave of change, one that will eventually be felt in almost every aspect of their lives at home, in the office, and in the world at large. This wave will profoundly transform our very identity as men at the same time it alters the industrial and social landscapes about us.

These changes will close off many of the familiar options men have enjoyed. But at the same time they offer men the promise of new opportunities and freedoms. For example, the additional earning power of a working spouse gives some men a sense of economic security and a more affluent lifestyle than they could ever have hoped to achieve on their own. Many men today feel better sharing, rather than shouldering, the responsibilities of modern life.

The trends are in place. They are probably irreversible. We men have a choice. Either we can resist—and be dragged along, kicking and screaming, flotsam on the currents of change. Or we can alert ourselves to the shift in directions and search for new values that will sustain us in these difficult times and allow us to participate fully in the new opportunities as they develop. But to do so, we must first recover that secretive half of our "self" we abandoned so many years ago.

WHAT PRICE GLORY?

Somewhere along the line we must realize that, as men, we have paid a price. Each of us can probably think of several parts of ourselves that we disowned. We snuffed them out. In the act of "being a man," what did we end up killing off in ourselves? Did we learn to squelch the desire to laugh, play, and feel? Did our fear that our secrets might get out effectively kill any childlike (as opposed to childish) behavior?

By choosing to go the way of concealment rather than that of openness, we men have too often brought upon ourselves sickness, misunderstanding, and self-alienation. We have had to pay a stiff price for the right to "be a man."

Compared with women, we men die younger, suffer a greater incident of fatal diseses (cancer, cirrhosis of the liver, pneumonia, and heart disease) as well as more migraines, ulcers, and alcoholism, commit suicide more often, and cope less effectively with stress.

In addition, large numbers of contemporary men pick loneliness as one of their chief burdens. "There's a loneliness for me and other men until we can share our feelings with each other," one California man admitted to writer Betty Friedan. "That's what I envy most about the women's movement—the way women share their feelings and the support they get from each other. Do you know how isolated and lonely and weak a man feels in that silence, never really making contact with another man?"

How are men supposed to know how to show their feelings when a chief message we have gotten from our early childhood has been that it is a sign of unmanly weakness to show our emotions? Remember Senator Ed Muskie, whose tears shed in public over a newspaper editor's sharp comments on his wife cost him his lead in the primaries of the 1972 presidential race?

In 1980, when *McCalls Magazine* conducted a reader survey on the state of modern marriage, one of the most common complaints the editors heard was in regard to the incommunicative husband. "We really don't communicate on an intimate level," one wife wrote in. "If I try to talk to him about my feelings or his feelings, he clams up. I feel very alone."

What we refuse to listen to time and time again is our women saying to us: "I love that you provide a secure income. But I don't want just your money. I don't want your vice-president-of-the-companyship. I want YOU! And all I'm getting is leftovers."

In recent years home computers have added a new twist to women's complaints about men's "silent routine." Many women have suddenly found themselves "computer widows," victims of what has now become known as the Silicon Syndrome, a new male hiding place.

For Joan, the wife of a vice-president of a manufacturing company, the last straw was her husband's decision to put a computer in their home so that he could work evenings on his company's records. "The only thing Bill understands is facts," she complained. "Feelings are as unknown to him as the far side of the moon. When he

installed that computer, I knew then it was time to get out
of my marriage." Joan walked out after twelve years of
marriage. "Now I will have more time to spend with my
computer," Bill joked weakly.

But Bill's plight is no joking matter. Was Bill hiding
from his wife, or simply running away from his feelings,
those emotions which his wife so desperately hoped could
once again renew their marriage?

MEN BEHIND WALLS

"There's no way to reach my husband, to know what is
really going on inside him," my friend Carol once confessed to me in exasperation. "He's built a wall ten feet
high around himself and then hung a KEEP OUT sign on it."

"Walls" are defenses we use to put distance between
ourselves and others. They are the major way we protect
our most private secrets and feelings. They help us hide
how easily hurt we are. We wall people out and ourselves
in, making elaborate rationalizations, justifications, and
excuses. Walls may be constructed from words or silence,
laughter or tears, fear or courage. Regardless of what
"bricks" we use in our walls, they all serve the same "security" function.

When we depend upon them, walls cut us off from other
people and reality. They keep our life partners, friends, and
children strangers. Having lived most of our lives behind
walls, we discover it is not easy to take them down. The
less secure we perceive ourselves to be, the more effort we
invest in our "defense spending." Debates rage on within
us, as they do in Congress, as we attempt to differentiate
the actual threats from the perceived threats and to justify

our expenditures of time and energy. As long as we men have secrets to keep, we will need walls between us and anyone who tries to get too close.

HOW WE SIDESTEP OUR FEELINGS

Feelings make up about one-third of our potential awareness. How we handle them is critical. Our feelings are our guideposts through life's processes—emotional impulses sent out to signal our basic psychological needs for protection, support, nurturance, and boundaries. But we were taught as boys to ignore or hide these signals from ourselves, and censor them with others.

Over the years we men have evolved a thousand and one clever ways to hide our feelings. We are masters at appearing emotionally unaffected and in control. Here are some of the common ploys we use.

- We rationalize a course of inaction by telling ourselves, "What good is it going to do to talk about it? That's not going to change anything!"

- We worry, worry, and worry, never facing what we really feel.

- We escape into new roles or hide behind old ones. ("Now wait just one minute—I'm the boss around here!")

- We take the attitude that "these feelings will pass" and shrug them off as unimportant.

- We keep busy.

- We change one feeling into another—by acting

angry when we are really hurt, for example, we create a smoke screen, diverting attention away from our true feelings.

- We deny the feeling outright.

- We put our feelings on hold—compartmentalize them or put them in a back file.

- We dull or dilute our feelings with diversionary tactics (silence, indifference, tiredness, laughter) or with drugs or alcohol.

- We perform a "thinking bypass"—replacing our feelings with thought and logic, intellectualizing and rationalizing our way around the feelings.

- We tense our bodies, so that we do not feel anything.

- We let our women do our feeling for us—reinforce women for being emotional and showing their feelings, so that we will not have to feel.

- We avoid situations and people who elicit certain feelings in us.

- We get sick or behave carelessly and hurt ourselves so that we have a reason to justify our feelings.

- We go crazy, so that somebody else has to take responsibility for our feelings.

Originally meant to inform us, our feelings instead have become a threat to us. We never really get to meet our feelings face to face because we are too busy defending ourselves. We hide behind the evening newspaper, in front of the television set, or in our work. When confronted, we retreat into silence or spend our leisure time in bars, where we can numb our feelings.

Relationships are the one area where we cannot afford to stamp our feelings TOP SECRET. If we wish to conduct effectively the daily business of a relationship and make important decisions about it, then we must bring into play our emotions. We cannot make decisions about what we want until, on a deeper level, we know what we feel. We cannot expect to get closer to somebody until we know how he or she feels. This, in turn, requires using those receptive feeling parts of our "selves," which, by the time we reach adulthood, have often taken an early retirement.

THE SECRET THAT ALMOST DESTROYED MY MARRIAGE

My own marriage is an excellent example of what happens when we fail to acknowledge a feeling and choose instead to keep it as a closely guarded secret. Early on, I decided to be the strong one. I assumed that it was my role in our relationship. So did my wife, Karen. Over the years, we've learned that playing that role did more damage than good to our marriage. Several years ago, something happened between Karen and me which showed us that I had to give up my "Superman" role or we would be in serious trouble.

A major strength of our marriage has always been our mutual decision to enjoy friendships with other men and women. Since we had been brought up with the illusion that we could meet *all* of each other's need, it was an important discovery when we learned friendships could be complementary to our own relationship. Each of us developed close friendships on our own with other men and women. We only asked of the other that such friendships not interfere with our marriage.

Over a period of several weeks, Karen developed a friendship with a man she had met at a professional conference. I have many women friends and associates whom I feel free to take to lunch, so Karen's relationship with her new friend was perfectly acceptable to me. But after meeting her friend for lunches and walks on the beach, I began to feel threatened. I kept my jealousy a secret and allowed the fear to build up inside of me.

One night everything just exploded. Karen and I had a fight about her friendship with this man. I ended up going for a slow drive up the coast. I thought to myself, "What if she's falling in love with this guy? She can't do this to me! I don't have to stand for this!"

That day was one of the few times in our marriage when I imagined myself being a single man again. I was angry. But that was just a cover. I later realized how hurt and scared I was. I hardly felt like the strong one at that point, even though a voice in my head told me I should be. I felt very confused.

I was not ready to face Karen when I returned home a few hours later and decided to sleep on the downstairs couch. After a while, she came down. She sat beside me. I remember not knowing exactly what my feelings were or what my response should be. I had never before felt this vulnerable around Karen. My anger was on the surface. But just below were my feelings of fear and pain.

Karen's words were soothing. "I understand that you feel threatened by my friendship with him," she tried to reassure me. "But I want you to know I am with you. He *is* my friend. And *yes*, I do enjoy his company. But I love *you*. Do you understand? *I love you*."

Before I knew it, I was in tears. For the first time in our relationship, I was aware that I could really lose Karen. I had invested my entire adult life in our partnership. But until that moment I had taken for granted the real importance our relationship had for me.

Karen asked if she could hold me. I wanted so badly to trust her, yet I fought her words. Seeing that I wanted her to hold me, but that I was frightened, Karen pulled me toward her. Being held calmed me. She was able to support me. I began to relax and feel a sense of relief.

All the time Karen held me, I was able to let myself go and take in her caring. So many times before, I had told myself that *I* was the only one who could be strong for *me*. It was *my* responsibility. I had never really given her my complete trust until then. Now that I had given her my trust, it felt right. I felt more emotionally honest than ever before.

We sat downstairs, talking, for what seemed a long time. Karen told me that sometimes in the past I had tried to get her to be "more like a man," as if holding back feelings was the only way to be strong. "When you cried tonight." Karen told me, "I got to see that you weren't really Superman. And that meant I did not have to be Superwoman."

Karen told me then that that evening was one of the most important moments in our marriage. By opening up my feelings to her, I had given her the opportunity to show me how strong she was and at the same time had shown her how much I honestly needed her.

"Don't you see?" Karen said, shortly before we fell asleep. "If I can't contribute something to you, I feel useless in our relationship. I need to feel needed and to be strong for you sometimes. Seeing this side of you makes me feel closer to you."

That night had changed our relationship. Karen understood me better. I had gained a deeper understanding of my own self. Our relationship had grown. Now I am free to be weak when I feel weak. And our partnership is more equal because there is room for both of us to be strong.

WHAT'S IN IT FOR US WHEN WE ACKNOWLEDGE OUR FEELINGS?

I learned then an important lesson. All too often we treat our feelings like the enemy and arm ourselves against them. But properly understood, feelings can be powerful allies.

How can our feelings help us?

- **Feelings motivate us.** Feelings challenge us to do our best and help us to get the job done. By plugging in to these feelings, we tap into an inexhaustible source of energy.

- **Feelings create a healthy environment for us.** If we deny or ignore our feelings for too long, our energy becomes depleted. By ventilating our feelings, we clear the air and make room for more healthy approaches to living. Expressing our feelings is still the single most effective way to reduce the level of stress in our lives.

- **Feelings connect us to other people.** Trusting our feelings and entrusting them to others builds strong bonds and relationships. When we relate to others on the level of feelings, we relate *with* them, not *to* or *at* them.

- **Feelings build confidence in us.** When we know intuitively that our decision feels right, we feel good about ourselves. We believe more in who we are and what we are doing. We feel more secure.

- **Feelings help us make the right decisions.** People in close touch with their feelings are more prepared to make difficult decisions and take important actions. We are ready for those times when we need to be at our intuitive best and cannot afford emotional "surprises." Feelings let us say with certainty, "I've got a gut feeling —this is the right decision!"

- **Feelings help us heal "old" and "new" wounds.** With emotional freedom, it is possible for us to understand and heal old wounds. All of us have been hurt and disappointed at some time in our lives, but we do not have to stay hurt. Feelings help us forgive others. None of us has to carry bad feelings around forever. Feelings help us to complete the unfinished business we have with other people and get rid of unnecessary guilt.

- **Feelings educate us.** Feelings teach us about ourselves. By experiencing new feelings, such as gentleness, we discover a new and better way to be effective. Being free to talk about our feelings in a safe and supportive environment shows us new sides of ourselves.

- **Feelings enliven us.** Feelings are an endless source of fresh, new energy in our lives. We are freer to play, enjoy music, move our bodies, laugh, and let go.

THREE STEPS FOR GETTING IN CLOSER TOUCH WITH OUR FEELINGS

Getting in touch with our feelings is the first important step in trading in our secrets and tearing down our walls. How can we reactivate or freshen up the feeling parts of ourselves? Where do we begin when, for so long, we may not have paid serious attention to our emotions? Here are three suggestions.

- **Keep in mind that our feelings are usually one- or two-word adjectives (angry, sad, scared, and happy).** Long verbal dissertations which begin, "I feel President Reagan's stand on the economy is . . ." are *thoughts*, not feelings. Make certain you are expressing feelings and not opinions.

- **We must learn to read our body's emotional signals.** Our bodies record feelings in several ways. We all experience our emotions differently. A recent incident from my own family illustrates this. My wife, Karen, and I were on the brink of an argument. She began, "How could you be so unfeeling and insensitive?" Within seconds I was preparing my usual defense, drawing heavily on logic. Our two daughters, ages six and nine, watched from the sidelines and began imitating us. We stopped, looked at each other, and started laughing. The kids, relieved at not having to sit through another one of Mommy and Daddy's silly fights, cheered their victory. As we were drawn closer together by our ability to laugh at ourselves, a very important question came up: "How do *you* feel your feelings?"

     We sat as a family and took turns explaining how we, as individuals, experienced our feelings. On one level, we all knew that we "felt" differently, but we had never taken time to understand how. It turned out that most of my feelings are like a tap on the shoulder. I notice something's there, but I have to think about it first before I'm willing to give it serious attention. Karen's feelings, she

explained, flood her entire body before she has a chance
to think about them. Jenna, age nine, told us that her
feelings sometimes appear bigger than her entire body.
And Stefie, our six-year-old, had trouble distinguishing
her feelings from the rest of her because they are such an
integral part of what she experiences.

Our sounds, images, sensations, and movements both
protect us and express what we feel. Our bodies are a
rich source of information about our feelings. By "reading" our body's signals, not only can we produce data
about how we feel, we can feel *better*.

- **We can talk out our feelings with a trusted friend.**
Talking about our feelings with a male or female friend
or a family member whom we trust is an excellent way
to get into closer touch with those feelings. The "rugged
individualist" in us still thinks something must be wrong
with a guy who needs to talk out his problems with
somebody else. Because we are not accustomed to ask
for help, many of us do not know how.

Here are practical steps that should make the act of
sharing our most deeply felt feelings much easier, less
stressful, and more productive.

The first thing we must remember is not to let the
pain get so big that it disables us. We must not wait until
we are emotionally half dead and bleeding to ask a
trusted friend out to lunch. The reality is that we *all* need
and benefit from support, caring, guidance, and understanding. Women know this. Most of them have friends
with whom they can talk about their feelings. Many men
do not.

Once we call one of our friends, we must explain
specifically what it is we want to discuss. This is impor-

tant. We can say something like: "This has really been a rough [or exciting] time for me, and I want to talk it over with you. Would you meet me for lunch tomorrow?" If the friend says, "Fine," then we are halfway home. If he or she cannot make it, we must not get discouraged. If we really want to talk to that person and our concerns can wait, then we can try to reschedule the meeting. If that is not possible, then we can call someone else.

After we meet with our friend, we should get straight to the point. Sometimes we may get frightened and revert to small talk. If we are scared, we can ask for reassurance from our friend: "Are you sure this is okay to talk with you like this?" Once we feel reassured, we should make clear how we want him or her to help: "I'd like you to listen to me without interrupting and then give me your impressions after I'm finished." Or we could say, "I'd like to know how *you* handled being a father for the first time"—or whatever situation is appropriate.

We should speak from our feelings, keep eye contact, and stay on the issue: "I'm really scared I won't be able to make enough money, what with the new house we just bought and the baby due next month."

We need to avoid giving or receiving "instant" advice, "quick fixes," or withdrawing prematurely from the conversation. We need to take time to explore our feelings, thoughts, and options thoroughly. We must be patient with ourself and our friend.

We need always to remember that we do not contact trusted friends and buddies just in time of need. We should learn to reach out to the people we want on our team and talk out our feelings with them on a regular basis.

Feelings are the key to unlocking men's secrets. We must learn first to recognize our feelings and then to express them to the appropriate people in a suitable way. Once we have done that, we will have gone a long way toward simplifying our life, sorting out our needs in various areas, and delineating a clear plan of action. Only then will we be living our life according to our own script, not someone else's.

Some of our most primary feelings about ourself, which make up our self-image, were derived from our relationship with our father. And that is what we want to take up in the next two chapters.

🎞🎞🎞🎞🎞🎞🎞🎞🎞 Chapter TWO

Life With Father: or, "Who Was That Masked Man?"

THE FATHER WITHIN US

When my Uncle Nathan was 70, he visited his father's grave tucked away in a corner of a cemetery in the Bronx. He stood there facing the headstone, the November wind ruffling his silver hair. Suddenly, his body started shaking. Tears streaked his face. "Dad, you never even put your arms around me," he sobbed, spilling out a secret grief that he had carried around with him all these years. "You never touched me. You never hugged me. Where were you when I needed you?"

It may surprise us to know that the most powerful common denominator influencing men's lives today is the relationship we had with our fathers. The events and circumstances may have taken place years, or even decades, ago. They may appear irrelevant to our lives in the present. But if we look beyond the surface, we will discover, as my Uncle Nathan did, that Dad is still very much with us today. Much of our behavior and many of our attitudes toward living can be traced to our fathers. Whether our dad was physically or psychologically absent, whether he died when we were young or is still alive at a ripe old age, whether we consider him a good father or a poor one, our fathers are in us. Every man hears the silent voice of his father inside his own head.

One of the most important clues to discovering who we really are lies in knowing who we were in relation to our fathers. One of the best-kept secrets for many men is the extent to which they allow themselves to be tied to their fathers, dead or alive. Of the hundreds of men I have surveyed over the years, perhaps 90 percent admitted they still had strings leading back to their fathers. In other words, they are still looking to their fathers, even though their fathers may have been dead for years, for approval, acceptance, affection, and understanding. And some, like my Uncle Nathan, will journey to their own graves with that secret longing unsatisfied.

Teaching us to be "real" men was the easy answer for an entire generation of fathers, most of whom were not secure enough in who they were to allow us to get close to them. Each of us has memories we cherish of those special moments when our fathers did allow us that direct contact. Unfortunately, the opportunities to get close enough to help us unscramble what it really meant to be a human being, not just to "be a man," were few. More often our stories uncover a deep yearning for Father's love and acceptance. "Our fathers wanted to raise us; but they didn't want to know us," was the way one man stated his disappointment. Many fathers held their sons at bay with anger, silence, busyness, harsh criticism, and indifference, asking only

that they be "good boys." "Just don't make trouble for your
mother and me," was their message. But "trouble" did
arise when our fathers did not respond to our emotional
needs.

In his novel *Dune*, Frank Herbert wrote: "There is probably no more terrible instant of enlightenment than the one
in which you discover your father is a man—with human
flesh."

American novelist Sherwood Anderson in his *Memoirs*
left behind a powerful account of one man's discovery and
acceptance of his father and the profound impact the experience had upon his subsequent life.:

"There came a certain night. Mother was away
from home when Father came in and he was alone.
He'd been off for two or three weeks.

"He came silently into the house. It was raining
outside. It may be there was church that night and
Mother had gone there. I had a book before me and
was sitting alone in the house, reading by the kitchen
table.

"Father had been walking in the rain and was very
wet. He sat and looked at me. I was startled, for on
that night there was on his face the saddest look I
have ever seen on a human face. For a long time he
sat looking at me, not saying a word.

"He was sad and looking at him made me sad. He
sat for a time, saying nothing, his clothes dripping.
He must have been walking for a long time in the
rain. He got up out of his chair.

"'You come on, you come with me,' he said.

"I was filled with wonder but, although he had
suddenly become like a stranger to me, I wasn't

afraid. We went along a street and out of the town.

"Finally we came to a pond. We stood at the edge. We had come in silence. It was still raining hard and there were flashes of lightning followed by thunder. My father spoke, and in the darkness and rain his voice sounded strange. It was the only time after we had left the house that he did speak to me.

"'Take off your clothes,' he said. Still filled with wonder, I began to undress. There was a flash of lightning. I saw that he was already naked.

"And so naked we went into the pond. He did not speak or explain. Taking my hand, he led me down to the pond's edge and pulled me in. It may be that I was too frightened, too full of a feeling of strangeness to speak. Before that night my father had never seemed to pay any attention to me.

"'And what is he up to now?' I kept asking myself. It was as though the man, my father I had not wanted as father, had got suddenly some kind of power over me.

"I was afraid and then right away, I wasn't afraid. It was a large pond and I didn't swim very well but he had put my hand on his shoulder. Still he did not speak but struck out at once into the darkness.

"He was a man with very big shoulder muscles and was a powerful swimmer. In the darkness I could feel the movement of his muscles. The rain poured down on us. The wind blew. There were flashes of lightning followed by the peals of thunder.

"And so we swam, I will never know for how long. It seemed hours to me. There was rain on our faces. Sometimes my father turned and swam on his back; and when he did, he took my hand in his large powerful one and moved it over so that it rested always on his shoulder. I could look into his face. There would be a flash of lightning, and I could see his face clearly.

"It was as it was when he had come earlier into the kitchen where I sat reading the book. It was a face filled with sadness. In me there was a feeling I had never known before that night. It was a feeling of closeness. It was something strange. It was as though I had been jerked suddenly out of myself, out of a world of the school boy, out of the world in which I was ashamed of my father, out of a place where I had been judging my father.

"He had become blood of my blood. He the stronger swimmer and I the boy clinging to him in the darkness. We went back along the road to the town and our house.

"It had become a strange house to me. There was the little porch at the front where on so many nights my father had sat with the men. There was the tree by the spring and the shed at the back. There was a lamp in the kitchen and when we came in, the water dripping from us, there was my mother. She smiled at us. I remember that she called us 'boys.' 'What have you boys been up to?' she asked, but my father did not answer. As he had begun the evening's experience with me in silence, so he ended it. He turned and looked at me, and then he went, I thought, with a new and strange dignity out of the room.

"He went to his room to get out of his wet clothes, and I climbed the stairs to my own room. I undressed in darkness and got into bed. I was still in the grip of the feeling of strangeness that had taken possession of me in the darkness of the pond. I couldn't sleep and did not want to sleep. For the first time I had come to know that I was the son of my father and that I would be a storyteller like him. There in the darkness in my bed in the room I knew that I would never again be wanting another father."

On that stormy night Anderson's father stopped running from himself and his own feelings. He faced himself and as a result was able to face his son. But even more important for his adolescent son was his act of inclusion. He gave him that precious moment of contact that all sons long for from their fathers. He allowed the young Anderson to get next to his essential humanity, to experience his maleness and his strength. His father gained a new dignity from the experience. And when fathers dignify themselves, they dignify us, their sons. From that night on the young Anderson had a father he could accept with pride. And having accepted his father, he could then accept himself. From that reconciliation his own life gained a new sense of direction and purpose. And as he grew older and developed into a writer, he understood that he had internalized the best features of his father.

Like it or not, our fathers have an enormous impact upon how we perceive ourselves as men and the male roles we eventually assume in life. If we take the time to search for him honestly in our own lives, most of us will be surprised to discover there is far more of our father in us than we ever suspected.

In order to come to terms with ourself, we must eventually come to terms with our father—and not just the father in real life who may or may not be still alive or emotionally unreachable, but also the father in ourself.

What do I mean by the "father in ourself"? That is the part in all of us which has taken over the role our father used to play or that we wanted him to play. If our father was a demanding perfectionist who continually criticized us, then we often treat ourself in the same manner, always finding fault with our actions.

We will want to examine closely our relationship with our father. Some of the things we will want to determine are:

Was our father capable of expressing love?

Did our father know how to express his love effectively or did he offer us his love in a form too abstract (such as money or expensive toys) for us to be able to appreciate it?

What did our father teach us about what it means to be a man?

Did we get the fathering we needed or do we still yearn for his approval and acceptance?

How has the relationship with our father affected our friendships with other men, our relationships with women, and the way we function in the workplace?

These are the crucial questions we will examine. But first let's do several exercises that will start us thinking about our fathers.

EXERCISE NO. 1

List three experiences you had as a boy with your father that provoked feelings of love, warmth, and security. Maybe it was sitting on his lap while he read you the Sunday funnies, teaching you how to throw a football, or taking you on a weekend fishing trip. Whatever they were, take a moment to record them here.

1. _____

2. _____

3. _____

List three experiences you had as a boy when your father hurt, disappointed, or angered you. Remember that day when he punished you for something your brother did, the fight he had with your mother, or that promise of a trip he failed to keep? Whatever the experiences, jot them down below.

1. _____

2. _____

3. _____

EXERCISE NO. 2

Do you have anything today that your father gave you when you were a boy? If so, what memories are associated with it? What feelings does it provoke in you today?

EXERCISE NO. 3

I am still tied to my father today in the following ways:

_____ financially
_____ for approval

_____ for my sense of self-esteem

_____ by fear that he will reject me unless I cater to him

_____ by competition

_____ by his criticism (I still run my life according to his values and opinions)

_____ by my rebellious defiance. That is, I am leading a lifestyle, working in a profession, or holding a set of political beliefs that I chose because it is the opposite of what my father would have wanted me to do.

Each of us must review our relationship with our father to understand our ties to him. My own story serves to illustrate that.

"WHO WAS THAT MASKED MAN?"

Do you remember watching *The Lone Ranger* on television or perhaps listening to his sagas on radio when you were a youngster? I certainly do. He was one of my earliest heroes. At the end of each episode, the Lone Ranger and Tonto rode out of town at full gallop, leaving behind a cloud of dust and a grateful crowd. Someone would always ask, "Who was that masked man?" And then someone else would reply, "Why, that was the Lone Ranger." From a distant hilltop we would hear the cry "Hi-yo, Silver, away!" The credits rolled and that was the end of the episode.

When I was a kid, something about that formula always bothered me, although then I could never quite put my finger on just what it was. Then a few years back when a

new Lone Ranger feature film appeared in the neighborhood theaters, I took my wife, Karen, and our two daughters to see the "big fella" ride again. Afterwards Karen and
I talked about the film and the importance of the mythic
figure of the Lone Ranger to my own childhood.

Suddenly, I understood what it was that had disturbed
me as a boy about the ending of all those Lone Ranger epi-
sodes. He was too much like my own father. Not that my
dad was a heroic, larger-than-life figure, single-handedly
defeating the forces of evil in this world. Rather, my father,
like the Lone Ranger, was always riding in and out of town.
And that was about all I ever saw of him. Off he went each
morning to catch the train into New York City. "Who was that
masked man?" I wanted to ask.

Who was my father, really?

I did not know. My father was a stranger to me in so
many ways. The world of his workplace was a mystery to
me. He was a very private man. I knew little about his
dreams, his fears, his feelings toward me. These were his
secrets. He rarely opened up to us. Did my father get anything from his children? I did not know. It was just like the
endings to those Lone Ranger stories. When that masked
man on his big horse with Tonto at his side rode away from
the town, did he ever get anything from the people whose
lives he had saved? Had they changed him in any way? Did
he ever see them again? We never knew. And, like the
Lone Ranger, my own father was in many ways a mysteri-
ous being to me. For years he had masked his true identity
behind a relentless commitment to his business and his exhaustion at the end of the workday.

This book was born out of important relationships in my
past. None has influenced me more than my relationships
with my father. I say "relationships" because we have

passed through so many phases together since those early years.

I secretly resented the fact that my dad put his business ahead of his family and gave so little of himself directly to me. I wanted far more fathering than he was able to give me. Yet I could never express this need to him. I was afraid. "Don't upset your father," my mother always cautioned us.

And so I grew up with the feeling that my father was unapproachable. My resentment built over the years as I saw the kind of fathering some of my buddies enjoyed in their homes. Their fathers spent time with them, taught them how to fix things, and helped them to develop hobbies. That's the kind of fathering I wanted so desperately. My longing to be loved by my father was my secret burden for years.

For a long time I believed that my dad had failed me in important ways. As his son, I could only see his faults, and so I denied him. It was not until much, much later that I discovered that by making my father the "bad guy" and judging his lifestyle as "wrong," I had made some important decisions about my own life. And in the process I had also denied a rich and vital part of my male heritage. I had denied the industrious, strong-willed, and confident part of my father that was in me. Most important, I had denied the love and gratitude I did have for my dad.

It was not until I was in my thirties that I realized I could not become truly free until I had come to terms with and expressed my feelings toward my father. Today I am proud of my father and the many qualities I share with him. We have become close buddies. Those parts of his life I do not agree with no longer pose a threat to my identity.

SEVEN KINDS OF FATHERS

Over the last decade I have talked to hundreds of men about their fathers. From our conversations I have learned that fathers come in seven forms or styles. Each one has its own predictable patterns and consequences. They are:

> **The Admiral Dad**
> **The Nice Dad**
> **The Professor Dad**
> **The Sad and Mad Dad**
> **The Marlboro Dad**
> **The Hardworking Dad**
> **The Loving-Present Dad**

A close look at the kind of fathering we received will yield valuable insights into how we see our role as a man today and perhaps suggest some major reasons for our emotional ups and downs. We want to determine what exactly we got from our father and what was lacking.

Let us keep in mind that the purpose in providing these categories is not to typecast our father as this or that. It is unlikely that our father will fit precisely into one category. However, they should help in identifying the nature of our father's influence as a man upon us.

THE ADMIRAL DAD

The Admiral Dad believes it is his "job" to "run" his family. He never really joins in the family activities because he is much too concerned with his responsibilities as the "head of the household." After all, he has to make certain that everything "runs smoothly." He sees to it that the other family members do their fair share in maintaining the family unit. The Admiral Dad keeps his wife and children at arm's length, giving orders, disciplining errant children, and supervising the family operations. He rarely relaxes or steps out of character. He runs a tight ship where everyone's role is clearly defined and everything is under strict control. The Admiral Dad thrives on consistency, a predictable routine to the daily schedule, and the loyalty of his family-crew. For the Admiral Dad, life is serious business *all the time*. He sees life as a matter of survival in a "dog-eat-dog" world. The Admiral is always in control. Always on duty. Always in a state of preparedness.

What we get from having the Admiral Dad as our father:

—a sense of consistency, order, discipline, and structure in our lives
—a respect for authority
—a dependency on externally imposed rules to create order within our lives
—an oversensitivity to authority
—a defiant rebelliousness against authority figures
—a false sense of security

What we are left seeking:

—parental warmth and affection
—intimate contact, closeness, and acceptance
—a need for constant expressions of approval
—a model of vulnerability

—a model of spontaneity
—a sense of individuality and our own uniqueness

THE NICE DAD

"Boy, is your dad nice," our buddies tell us over and over again. The Nice Dad probably does not show much of his deeper feelings. But he is generally agreeable, easygoing, and pleasant. He is just "a regular guy" going about the business of life. Concealed in his evenness and passivity is a man who refuses to risk or invest himself emotionally through a serious commitment *in depth* to others. The Nice Dad holds himself back because he has never learned to trust himself with his innermost thoughts and feelings. Often when shown how to display his affections, he will go along. But he will never quite get that feeling right. Being such a "pleaser," the Nice Dad is often prone to passive-aggressive behavior and occasional outbursts of temper.

What we get from having the Nice Dad as our father:

—a cooperative, patient, and easygoing style of relating to others
—an unclear sense of limits and boundaries
—a casual and superficial style of communication
—a "play it safe" attitude toward relationships, even close ones

What we are left seeking:

—closeness, contact, and depth in our relationships
—a sense of how far we can grow and prosper
—a model of assertiveness
—those skills necessary to resolving conflicts

THE PROFESSOR DAD

The Professor Dad believes it is his job to teach his children well. This dad is anxious to make certain his children are doing the "right" thing. He thinks in terms of absolutes. There is a "right" way and a "wrong" way to everything. He seizes upon every possible opportunity to lecture his children (or anyone else, for that matter). The Professor Dad views himself as an expert on everything. He enjoys making others look foolish by exposing their supposed ignorance. He will embarrass his children and undermine their self-confidence, underestimating their knowledge and skills. Eventually, people tune him out because he is not tuned in to them. Because he is out of touch with his children's real needs and abilities, they in time grow distant from him. But the Professor Dad never stops. He plods on until there is finally no one left to listen to him, except the family cat or dog.

What we get from having the Professor Dad as our father:

—a mind full of instructional information that plays on in our head like an endless tape, "Dad's Comprehensive Guide to Growing Up Right"

—tuning-out skills

—radar to detect concerned but irrelevant advice

—a sense that we never really "related" to or were touched by our father

—a voice inside us that constantly criticizes us for never being "perfect"

—feelings of self-doubt and inferiority which give us an overall sense of low self-esteem

What we are left seeking:

—people who will accept with confidence our intelligence and trust us to make the right decisions
—people who will relate to us without bullying us intellectually
—people who will tell us what we should do because we were so dependent upon the Professor at one time doing this for us

THE SAD AND MAD DAD

The Sad and Mad Dad, unperceived to his family, is deeply troubled and unhappy inside. He simply does not enjoy his life. But he never complains. Instead, he swallows his pain—that is, until it erupts into anger. His family receives the brunt of his pent-up feelings of tension, frustration, unhappiness, and self-pity. They feel intimidated and unsafe around him. The Sad and Mad Dad frequently feels guilty and as a result often resorts to alcohol as an escape from the pain within. He is unwilling to ask for or receive help. He lives on, feeling stuck in his job, paying the bills, and making excuses for his bad moods at home. Frequently, the Sad and Mad Dad will leave his family, abdicating his responsibility for everyone and everything. But his family has already experienced his psychological absence for a long time. And so, in many ways, his departure comes as a relief.

What we get from having the Sad and Mad Dad as our father:

—a model of depression and unhappiness
—a burden of guilt, as we go through life thinking

that we were in some obscure way at fault for our father's problems
—a model for parents' suffering in an unhappy marriage
—a sense of loss and abandonment
—a feeling of never being loved or wanted by our father
—a "call to duty" as the "little man of the house" when Dad is drunk or after he has left home

What we are left seeking:

—to be the "good father" our own father could never be to us
—a need to prove that all men are really no good
—to repress our own anger and unhappiness, so that we will not turn out to be like our father

THE MARLBORO DAD

Astride his horse, riding into the sunset, the Marlboro Dad sits tall in his saddle. He is successful and secure. He gives the appearance of a man who has everything worked out satisfactorily. This dad is impeccable. Occasionally, Mom gets up on her tippy-toes to brush some lint off the jacket of his three-piece suit. But that is about as "imperfect" as we will ever see him. The Marlboro Dad is constitutionally strong and self-reliant and an excellent provider. He is the first one up in the morning and the last to bed at night. The Marlboro Dad has an exaggerated sense of the meaning of masculinity, which he defines in narrow, traditional terms. He often sees his son as little more than an extension of his own ego. He pushes hard for his son to be a success in school, in sports, with girls, and at work because it throws glory on his role as father. Marlboro Dads can be cruelly judgmental of their sons. They give their affection only when they think their sons have "earned" it.

What we get from having the Marlboro Dad as our father:

— a model of responsibility and strength
— a mystique about powerful males
— a sense of despair as we wonder, "How am I ever going to follow *his* act?"

What we are left seeking:

— to be "as good as he was" by competing with his standards
— to climb on a tall horse for our family
— a sense of rebellion as we throw off everything that our father represented for us
— failure rather than success, so that we do not have to compete with our father
— to have our life under control *all* the time
— to prove our masculinity through the accumulation of wealth, power, and sexual conquests
— a dependency on women to express those emotions we deny to ourselves
— attention to our accomplishments

THE HARDWORKING DAD

The Hardworking Dad may be a devoted, loving provider, doing his utmost on behalf of his family's security and comfort. In exchange for the "good life," this dad overworks himself and uses his home chiefly for sleep and rest. What energy he has left after twelve hours in the office six days a week is not enough to nourish his family. Workaholic dads are so focused on achievement that they forget their human limits. Stress in their lives is met with —you guessed it!—still more work. This carries with it an alienation and isolation from the joys of human life. Heart disease, family problems, ulcers, physical and emotional exhaustion, and feelings of estrangement from their wives and children are only a few of the high costs that the Hardworking Dad inflicts upon himself.

What we get from having the Hardworking Dad as our father:

- —a model of self-sacrificing behavior
- —the ethic that "life is work"
- —a father who usually suffers from chronic stress-related problems and dies prematurely
- —a sense of guilt when we are on vacation, having fun, or not working "hard enough"

What we are left seeking:

- —direct contact with a father who could have taught us what it meant to be a human being
- —a model of health, balance, and good management of personal time that we could use for guidance in our own life
- —an image of well-rested parents who make time for intimacy, leisure, and recreational activity

THE LOVING-PRESENT DAD

The Loving-Present Dad is, for most of us, the idealized version of the man we all wanted for our father but only a few of us actually got. He was psychologically and physically present because he chose to give his role as father priority in his life. With this dad, we felt that he really knew and understood us as well as loved us. We, in turn, knew and loved him. The Loving-Present Dad was there as a model of strength and sensitivity, firmness and flexibility. Not only did he put his son's interests uppermost, but he was adept at seeing things from his son's point of view. He was a man who enjoyed life to the fullest and shared that joy with his son. The Loving-Present Dad was a true pal to us. He was there when we needed him. He may not have been perfect, and we might have had our disagreements with him on occasion. But the conflicts were resolved amicably. The Loving-Present Dad never pushed his authority on us. He helped us form our own values. Sometimes the Loving-Present Dad was the father of a close buddy up the street. We would then try to imagine what it would have been like to have him as our dad.

What we get from having the Loving-Present Dad as our father:

— love, warmth, and understanding
— a living example of a man who lives in harmony with himself and his family
— support and backing to grow up
— unconditional acceptance and appreciation for the unique person whom we are

Which of the above types of fathers best describes the one you had?

_____

Before we continue, it will be useful to do several exercises that will help us understand more fully the relationship we had with our father and its impact upon us as an adult.

This is important. Meeting our father as an adult frequently means we must overcome the fears, hopes, idealizations, expectations, grudges, and judgments we have made about him in the past.

EXERCISE NO. 4

Let's take an inventory of our expectations for our own father. Sons are as demanding of their fathers, as fathers are of their sons. So let's do a quick checklist of the expectations we, as a son, had of our father and discover which of those expectations were met and which were disallowed (the "yes" or "no" portion). Perhaps too many of our expectations went unmet. Then, as an adult, we may be looking to other men to satisfy those longings from our youth.

I wanted from my father:

_____attention: yes_____ no_____

_____approval: yes_____ no_____

_____recognition: yes_____ no_____

_____love: yes_____ no_____

_____guidance: yes_____ no_____

_____his time: yes_____ no_____

_____close physical contact: yes_____ no_____

_____companionship: yes_____ no_____

_____a sports partner: yes_____ no_____

_____a mentor: yes_____ no_____

other: _____ yes_____ no_____

        _____ yes_____ no_____

        _____ yes_____ no_____

EXERCISE NO. 5

My father fulfilled my expectations in the following ways:

    1. _____

    2. _____

    3. _____

My father failed to meet my expectations in the following ways:

    1. _____

    2. _____

    3. _____

MAN TO MAN

Sometimes we can best learn from one another by hearing the unedited, uncut versions of what happened to us in

our past. There is insight and healing in the mere telling of
a story for both the talker and the listener. The stories of
our lives with our fathers delight, sadden, and fascinate us.
Embedded in those stories are our earliest and most basic
teachings about how to be a man. So let us hear what
several men, like yourself, have had to say about their experiences with their fathers.

"On a blustery winter afternoon in 1944, my father waited with me in Penn Station for the train that
would take me away to the Army center where I
would begin my military service. He looked at me
with tears clouding his eyes, hugged me tightly, and
told me goodbye in a choked voice. Then, wanting to
give me something that was his, he took off his
watch and handed it to me.

"As I walked toward the train, I looked back at
my father, who was waving gently and sadly to his
17-year-old son. Suddenly, I noticed that several people were watching us with bemusement. I sensed
then that such an intimate farewell was perhaps un-
conventional between a father and son. My feeling
was emphasized by a family scene occurring to my
right. Another father, gravely smiling, gave his boy a
firm pat on the back and said, 'I'm proud of you.' I
wondered, as I observed this formality between father and son, how they *really* felt about each other.
And I thought how different it was—how different it
had always been—with my father."

Dr. Lee Salk, psychologist,
in *My Father, My Son*

"My father was never very emotional. I don't
think I ever hugged my father. He never told me he

loved me, and he never said he was sorry. We just never really got along. He smashed my head down in a plate of spaghetti one time.

"He never showed any emotional love. Just maybe if I needed money for school, he would give it. Mom always told me that my father couldn't show these kinds of things but he'd try in other ways. I needed emotional love and support. I never, ever got that, and I think my life shows that I was always trying to get it with older males.

"When he got extremely frustrated, he'd throw something, or cuss and walk out. And I've got some of that in me, too. I burst into these rages and walk out and throw things; and I *hate* that part about me, that part that is my father."

> Mark Chapman,
> the killer of singer John Lennon
> (quoted in *McCalls Magazine*)

"I remember when I was a kid how I loved to wrestle with my father. He was never one to touch me or hug me much. Our wrestling matches were my way of getting physical contact from him."

> John, 32,
> an accountant in Chicago

"My dad was 40 when I was born. I really see that as important. He was an old forty. When I was growing up, my father spent a lot of time with me. He worked hard and was successful and wealthy. I knew he loved me a lot. But he was overweight. I never wanted my friends to meet him because he was so fat. I loved him. But he also embarrassed me. Those conflicting feelings were hard for me to handle as a kid."

Don, 32,
an owner of a small business in Denver

"One day when I was a small boy during the lean days of the Depression, my father got me up before dawn to go duck hunting. He had been a car sales-man but nobody was buying De Sotos that year, so he finally found a job in a gas station. That morning he carried a shotgun he had borrowed from a friend 'to shoot a little something for our table.'

"It was first light when we settled ourselves into the reeds at the edge of the lake. Almost immediately a wave of thirty of the big birds passed high over-head, filling the air with their haunting, unforgettable honking. I can still hear it now, when I set my mem-ory on it. I had never seen before such majestic, pur-poseful birds, formed into a perfect aerial V.

"I looked at my father as he uttered a little groan of awe. He stood transfixed as the flock flew across the sunrise. 'Canadian snow geese,' he finally said, the shotgun still at his feet.

"We never saw another bird the entire morning. But driving home, Dad appeared strangely uncon-cerned that we were coming home empty-handed without fifty cents in our pockets. 'Weren't they something?' he exulted.

"I don't remember what we ate that night. But I do remember that my father felt that beauty had an important place in a man's life. I have never forgot-ten the lesson of that day."

Jim Sanderson, syndicated columnist,
in his book, *Men, Women and Love*

"Dad always found time for me. Our chief connection was baseball. We were both Brooklyn Dodger fans. He always took me to their home games. My dad knew a lot of the ball players and introduced them to me. I can't tell you the excitement I felt as a boy at meeting those players. It was the highlight of my life then. But when I got to be 14 or 15, the connection weakened and we drifted apart. The Dodgers and baseball were the major way we connected. And that is true, even today. It has been over twenty years but my father still sends me articles about the Dodgers that he clips out of magazines and newspapers. In his last letter he sent along a clipping from *The Wall Street Journal* about some company that was reprinting all the old baseball cards. He said he had ordered me a set for the Dodgers of 1952.

"My father taught me to work hard, be responsible, be honest with others, love the Dodgers—and to play my feelings close to my chest. As we have grown older together, I find I really love my father. And I know he loves me. But we can never bring ourselves to express that love verbally. Even when I hug him, he can't hug me back. Yet I know he loves me. If I had one wish, it is that Dad would hug me before he dies."

Robert, 39,
an investment counselor in Miami Beach

"My father was an outdoorsman. I took after him in that respect. I look on myself as the ultimate outdoorsman. I lived in the Montana wilderness for four years in a primitive cabin. I shot three elk in two years. And I am one hell of a fly-fisherman. My father knows all this. And yet I have never received from him any recognition for my achievements as an outdoorsman. He has always been so damn distant."

Rick, 33,

a ranger with the U.S. Park Service in Oregon

"I grew up on a farm in Iowa during the Depression. I never had the choice then that kids have today. In those tough years I got up in the early morning and started on my chores. They had to be done, regardless of the weather. My father taught me self-sufficiency at an early age.

"When I was in eighth grade, my father injured himself in an accident and became an invalid. My tenure as a child was over. I was a man. It was now up to me to take over the farm, run it, and get the crops in. I'd go down to the bank when we needed money and tell them how much money we had to borrow. The banker would give me a note to take home and have Dad sign it. I was hiring, firing, and paying people, and selling our crops when I was fifteen. So I made a fast transition from boy to adult.

"My dad took five years to recover from his injuries. We were very close in that time, very supportive of each other. Eventually, after he recovered his health, we farmed together. That was great for a while. But I felt that I was not my own person. So I set out to look for my own farm. I ended up in a little town about sixty miles away. I decided to buy a house but I wanted Dad to check it out first. So I called him up and said, 'Dad, I found this terrific house I want to buy. Will you please come and take a look at it?' He said, 'No, son, I don't need to look at it. You're buying it.'

"I knew right then it was all over. I was 22 or so at the time. Dad was not being cruel. He was just saying that it was time for me to stand on my own two feet. 'Trust yourself; do what you think is right,' was his message to me. That was a big influence on my life. My father remained my best friend right up to the time of his death ten years later."

John, 56, a farmer in Iowa

Chapter THREE

Reaching Out to Father

THE FATHER IN OUR HEART

The first week of September 1983, I was away from San Diego to conduct one of my Alive and Male seminars in another large western city. After a particularly productive session which included men from all across the state, I appeared as the featured guest on a local radio talk show. The host had asked in advance that we focus our discussion on father-son relationships. Two days before, the Russians had shot down a Korean Airlines 747 that had intruded into its airspace. Both of us expected that this dramatic break in foreign news would dominate the exchange afterwards when listeners called in with their questions and responses.

But that never happened. After I had talked at length about the importance of a man's relationship with his father as a major influence on his life, the host of the talk show suddenly opened up and talked for the first time to another person about his painful childhood with an alcoholic father.

"I have no relationship with my father," he confessed, unburdening himself on the air of his deepest and most painful secret. "I hate the man and always have. He has been a lousy father to me. I have not seen him for five years. I do not miss him. And when he dies, I will not go to his funeral."

The response from the listening audience was incredible. Dozens of people called in during the "open phones" hour. A few wanted to talk about the recent Russian atrocity, but most were more upset about the host's comments on his father. They urged him not to disown his own father, whatever his sins.

"For God's sake, if you've not seen your father in five years, try to achieve a reconciliation," one man pleaded. "We all change in time. Maybe you two can get talking again. You may hate him now. But ten years from now, after he is dead, you will kick yourself for not having made one last effort."

The experience dramatically brought home to me an important lesson. Initially, we all want to love and be loved by our father. When his love for us is withdrawn, discovered to be highly conditional, fades away, is lost, or simply has never been made available to us, we respond in turn by cutting off our expression of love for him. We close our hearts to our father. We deny that we still have a need for his love and approval. But we still carry around, buried secretly deep inside us, the child we once were who wanted so desperately his father's love. Unconsciously we still seek it—in success, wealth, status, or the approval of other men. Some men turn to God, the "ultimate father." Others seek their fathers in the workplace.

How much better for us if we can move beyond the

stage in which we put our father's face on our boss, a
brother, an uncle, a teacher, a close male friend, or older
men in general. We need to stop licensing other people to
approve us, to accept our bids for their love.

John, 38, is a successful doctor of family medicine in
San Diego; his search for his father's approval determined
his entire professional life. It was a major factor behind his
decision to seek medicine as his career. Until John came to
me, he had never talked about his feelings on this painful
matter, not even to his wife.

"I made up my mind when I was quite young to seek a
career as a doctor although at the time I could never understand why that particular profession seemed so attractive to
me over others I had investigated," John reflects today. "It
was not until much later that I realized the importance of
my father to my selection of a career. Dad never gave me
much approval when I was a boy. In fact, he was always
critical of me. I couldn't do anything right in his eyes. I
tried so hard to get that man's approval when I was a kid.
But he just couldn't bring himself to say, 'Good job, John,
I'm proud of you.' I realize now that I started looking elsewhere, outside the home, for the approval I wanted from
Dad but never got. And that's the reason I ended up in
medicine. Patients are always so appreciative when you
help them. I get lots of positive stroking from them. But I
sometimes wonder how different my life would be today
and what my career would have been had my father been a
different sort of man."

There are many men today who, like John, are driven
by secret needs left unsatisfied by their fathers. Sometimes
the search for Father can take bizarre forms. Jim, 42, a
professor of literature at a large East Coast university, ten
years ago suddenly started obsessively collecting and read-

ing Walt Disney comic books from the 1940s and 1950s. At the time he thought it was simply nostalgia for an earlier era. But then he found his comic books at the center of a series of reoccurring dreams in which he went from used bookstore to used bookstore looking for his comic books. He would awake just as he found them. It was not until Jim was in therapy a number of years later that he understood the importance of his comic books.

"My mother and father divorced when I was three," Jim remembers today. "My father stayed in Houston. Mother returned to her hometown of Chicago. Father came to visit several times. Usually, he took me and my brother out to an afternoon movie and then to dinner. Before taking us home, he bought us each a comic book. I always wanted one of the Disney comics. Then I didn't see Father again. He died of a stroke when I was ten. When I was 32, I was up for tenure consideration and under a great deal of stress. I needed a father then to reassure me that everything was all right. That was when I started collecting the comic books and dreaming about them. The comics had come to represent, at a subconscious level, Father. I had never admitted to myself how much the loss of my father had meant to me when I was a kid."

Remember:

- **We must retrieve that part of us we have sent in search for our father.**

- **It is only after we have come to terms with our search for our father that we can begin the search for our own self.**

Because there is a validation of us as human beings that can come only from our fathers, few things we can do will give us greater satisfaction and peace of mind than to effect a reconciliation with an estranged father. That is the only way we can still the incessant cries of the small child that many of us carry around inside us.

And we must not fall into the trap of thinking that it is all over and there is nothing more we can do simply because our father is no longer alive. As I shall explain later, a loving reconciliation with your father is always possible, even though he may have been dead for years.

The rewards of such a reconciliation are enormous, not the least of which is the freedom to be our own man unencumbered by the burdens of the past that compel us to chase ceaselessly after ghosts. We want to regain control of our lives.

EXERCISE NO. 1

First, let's begin to determine the extent to which you may still be tied to your father in one way or another. Answer "yes" or "no" to the following questions:

1. Do you struggle with authority figures, always challenging them and feeling victimized at the end of the confrontations? _____

2. Do you avoid contact with older men, judging them as "too old" or uninteresting for you? _____

3. Do you find yourself acting shy or boyish in the presence of men older than yourself? _____

4. Are you competitive and/or defensive around older men? _____

5. Do you fantasize much about your struggles or relationships with other men—the boss, your brother-in-law, buddies? _____

6. Do you follow authority blindly? _____

7. Are there men in your life you would do anything to please? _____

8. Do you avoid thinking about your father? _____

9. Do you often feel that someone is treating you just like your father did and you do not like it? _____

10. Do men who remind you of your father bring out anger in you or make you feel vaguely ill at ease? _____

An abundance of "yes" responses to the above questions would indicate the real possibility that you have stronger ties to your father than you may have acknowledged to yourself.

EXERCISE NO. 2

Our imagination can be a powerful tool in our search for a better, stronger, freer self. For years we have probably tuned out the "little boy" so many of us carry around inside us. We refuse to listen to him. We make up all sorts of excuses. "I'm too busy," we tell ourselves. Or: "That little six-year-old in me is just too damn silly. He embarrasses me!"

I am going to ask you to take some quiet moments now to listen to that little boy inside you. Don't try and change him. Don't argue with him. Just listen to what he is trying to tell you.

Remember: if that little boy in us can feel understood, the experience will be one of the most healing and educational ones we, as human beings, can have.

Now I want you to use your imagination to get in touch with the little boy who was you twenty, thirty, or forty years ago.

First, get a mental picture of him. What does he look like? How old is he? What is he doing? What row does he sit in the classroom? (I never cease to be amazed at the number of men for whom a seat at the front or the rear of the classroom was a major source of happiness or anguish in their boyhood.)

Now listen to his message. What does he want from his father? It may be something very simple. It may not appear important. But listen to it. You may hear, "Daddy, hold me." Or: "Daddy, don't hurt me." That little boy's need is a very real one, and you may still be looking for it today.

Write below or in your journal the little boy's message.

EXERCISE NO. 3

The search for Father often ends when we feel recognized and appreciated for who we are and what we have accomplished. Below I have listed some validating messages that men have told me they received from their fathers or wanted to hear. Put down a "yes" or "no" for each one, depending on whether or not your father said it to you.

_____ "I'm proud of you, son."
_____ "I think you've grown into a fine man, son."

_____ "I forgive you, son."

_____ "Please forgive me, son."

_____ "I love you, son."

_____ "You've been a good son to me."

_____ "Thanks, son."

others   *(write them in)*

_____ _____

_____ _____

_____ _____

EXERCISE NO. 4

If you have more "no" responses than "yes" ones to the preceding exercise, then consider bringing the matter up directly with your father. You might start out by saying, "Dad, I've given a lot of thought recently to our relationship. It would mean a great deal to me if we could talk about it."

Remember—do not accuse, blame, judge, criticize, or attack him. You do not want a confrontation. But, on the other hand, do not beat around the bush with him. Go straight to the point.

During the course of your conversation, tell him about the list of validating messages. You might even engage him in a discussion about how he would have liked to be validated by his own father.

Then ask him directly to say positive things about you, as a father to his son, so that you can know how he feels about you. Tell him those areas which have special meaning to you. For example, you might ask him, "Dad, it would mean a great deal to me if you could say something about how proud you felt when I joined the Peace Corps."

Let him respond without interruption. Open up your receptive channels.

Note below or in a separate journal your father's responses.

EXERCISE NO. 5

Now ask your father to write in the space below or in your journal a validation and acknowledgment of you, his son. You might ask your father to do it on your birthday, as his gift to you. Have him record here or on tape, his appreciation for you, his son.

EXERCISE NO. 6

We make a million excuses to postpone having to face our father. The best way, I guess, is simply to wait for him to die. But beyond our fear, righteousness, stubbornness, pride, and rationalizations lie a thousand opportunities for us to do something about our relationship with our living father. Here are four that will take about as much of our time as reading the Sunday paper:

1. Place a phone call to him right now.
2. Write him a letter today.
3. Plan a visit to see your father or have him visit you.
4. Make a symbolic gesture of love, such as sending him a card (humorous?) or a special gift.

EIGHT BENEFITS OF A RECONCILIATION WITH FATHER

1. Our goal should always be to gain more control over our lives. Hence, the importance of achieving a reconciliation with our father. It will allow us to be our own man, not our father's man.

2. When fathers and sons are reconciled, the other family members are inspired to clean up their own relationships, not only with Dad but with Mom and brothers and sisters. The family grows stronger and continues on a more positive note. It becomes easier for all its members to express their feelings of love and forgiveness, to communicate more openly, and to resolve their differences.

3. Reconciliation with our father allows us to achieve a communication with him that we would never have believed possible before. We no longer allow the old, negative beliefs or the ur-

gent searching to color all our relationships with
him. Our time together is uncluttered by impotent
rage, unrealistic expectations, or the desire to
change our father.

4. The "fringe benefits" of a love relationship with
   our living father are unlimited. We have opened
   the doors to each other's lives and the richness
   that comes in sharing special moments, support-
   ing one another's goals, assisting one another in
   times of need, and generating newfound affection
   for one another. The power of being understood
   by your father and of understanding your father
   can be used to heal, educate, and affirm one's
   self.

5. Face to face, man to man, you are your father's
   equal. You no longer need to "prove" yourself by
   doing "manly" deeds. Your father accepts and
   loves you for the person you are. The great equal-
   izer, in this case, is not money, title, or power but
   patient understanding.

6. The confidence born of a loving, healthy father-
   son relationship sets a precedent for other relationships in the lives of both the father and the
   son. The son will relate positively to older male
   authority figures from a position of strength and
   ease. The father will relate to younger men without feeling any threat of one-upmanship.

7. As many of us reach the height of our careers, our
   fathers are winding theirs down. When we are at
   the peak of our physical powers, our fathers are
   experiencing a decline of theirs. On the other

hand, as many of our fathers are letting go of their "harness," we, their sons, are hardening our line of approach to living. We can learn from the unique textures each season brings as we partake of each other's lives. Autumn remembers spring, as spring looks on autumn's rich colors.

8. Bringing the search for Father to a satisfying end conserves valuable time and energy. Resources otherwise consumed by the "dad hunt" may be directed toward living fully in the present.

THE MYTH OF IMPERFECT FATHERS, PERFECT SONS

Before I flew back East several years ago for the specific purpose of achieving a reconciliation with my own father, I was secretly afraid of him. I was afraid, too, of my feelings for him. I was fearful he would reject me, invalidate my feelings toward him, and fail me. I knew that if that happened, it would leave me with a sense of emptiness and humiliation. At the time I was not fully conscious of these feelings. But they were there. I just knew that until that day I had never been prepared to take the risk of exposing myself to my father. When we were together, I refused to be vulnerable around him. I played it safe. I protected myself. Mother was my favorite. I only gave Dad a formal nod now and then. I had him typecast as the heavy. So long as it held up, it justified the distance between us. Underneath I longed for a closer relationship with my father. But I never thought it would be possible. It was safer for me to believe that.

Shortly before my visit back East, I saw the movie *Tribute*. It changed my outlook. For the first half of the movie Jack Lemmon's character is badgered by his hostile son, who continues to bludgeon him over the head with his failures as a father. "You divorced Mom." "You never had time for me." "You pushed me to grow up." Lemmon takes it, takes it, and takes it. But then, knowing he is dying from cancer, Lemmon explodes at his son: "Damn you! Did you ever stop to think you were hardly a perfect son? Did it ever strike you that maybe I was terribly disappointed in you?" His anger is loaded with passion and vulnerability. Perhaps for the first time in their relationship, this man shows his son the true feelings inside him.

As I watched the story unfold, I suddenly found myself getting all choked up and teary-eyed. I realized then that it was me on the screen. All these years I had wanted my father to be vulnerable to me. And yet I never allowed myself to be vulnerable around him. I had to wait until my thirties before I realized the dreadful truth about myself—that I was as distant from my father as I perceived him to be from me. The next day I booked a flight back East for the specific purpose of seeking a reconciliation with my father.

In order to gain this reconciliation I had first to accept certain realities about the fathering I had received and then to let go of the grudges against Dad I had carried around for all those years. As a child, I had wanted my father to teach me all those great things that a boy wants to learn— how to play baseball, build a cart, use a camera. But my father was too busy to spend that kind of time with me. I really hurt inside when I saw the affectionate attention some of my buddies received. They had special relationships with their fathers that I seemed to be missing out on with my own dad.

I later had to accept that my father loved me in his own way. And there were more good times than I had remembered. The fathering I got was not the fathering I would have ordered up. But it was my reality to accept. And that is a first and major step toward any reconciliation between a son and his father.

EXERCISE NO. 7

Parent-child relationships are a two-way street. Even as kids, we make decisions which make us more or less approachable to our parents. We learn effective ways to keep them at a distance. Sometimes we keep them there for a lifetime. Be honest with yourself. Check off the ways you might have used to keep your father at a distance.

_____ acting dumb
_____ acting like you knew it all
_____ deliberately defying him
_____ not listening to him
_____ spacing out on drugs
_____ siding with Mother in family arguments
_____ making excuses to avoid contact
_____ typecasting him
_____ competing with him

THE EXPECTATIONS GAME

Another game sons play with fathers centers on expectations. What did we expect from our dads? On what basis did we form our expectations? Did we expect our dad to be a Robert–*Father Knows Best*–Young kind of father, always at home, always involved, wise and understanding, able to solve all our problems within a thirty-minute time frame? Or did we see our dad as a Santa Claus, appearing only on special occasions bearing an assortment of gifts and goodies? Was he invincible, like Superman, or a pushover, like Clark Kent? Or was he both, depending upon the situation?

Are we still holding on to these childhood expectations of Father? If so, it is likely that we have been disappointed over and over again by our fathers.

In reality, most of our fathers were both weak *and* strong, involved *and* detached, magical *and* mundane, because *our fathers are human*. And that we often forget. Expecting our father to be one way all the time, stereotyping him into the "Perfect Dad," ensures only that we will be disappointed. And that is the easy way out of a complex dilemma. We can allow ourselves to be disappointed by setting up unrealistically high expectations of the behavior we expect from our father. Or we can face the reality that he is human. And that means accepting the fact that he has faults and frailties as well as strengths and positive attributes. Stacking the evidence against him and making him into the "Bad Guy" is yet another way we have of not having to face *our* own human limitations.

A common variation on this game involves sons of fathers who were extraordinarily successful in some particular pursuit. They go through life fearful they will never measure up to their fathers' high standards. One of my clients is an accountant with a Ph.D. from one of the country's top graduate schools and an income of $150,000 a year. And yet he secretly thinks of himself as a failure. His own father was for over forty years a family physician in a small community in New England. He was known and beloved throughout the region for his selfless dedication to the well-being of others. In his own quiet way his father was a great and extraordinary man. Hundreds of people attended his funeral. His son has always felt inadequate in comparison to his father and has lived his life in the fear that he will never be as good a man as he.

THE HOSTAGE GAME

The Hostage Game is another ploy we often use when we refuse to accept our own responsibility for a fractured father-son relationship. In this game we adopt a defensive posture in life and hold our father psychological hostage to his past behavior. There are several ways we do this.

- We make our father into the "Bad Guy." We put a black hat on his head. In this posture we ascribe our father's behavior to his essentially "bad" nature. We convince ourself that he is inherently evil and cannot change. Often we pick up on other family members' anger and sense of powerlessness against our father and align with them against him.

- We make what our father did unforgivable. In effect, we hold court, become his judge and jury, and give him a lifelong sentence never to be commuted. We cast him off. We make no attempt to understand what lay behind his behavior. Behind this posture toward Father is almost always a son who still sees himself as a victim in his life. ("Dad deserted me." "Dad physically assaulted me." "Dad was an alcoholic." "Dad cheated on Mom.") Because we never found a way to reconcile ourself to what happened back then, we cannot forgive our

father for what he did. To do so would mean com-
muting his sentence.

- We foul up our own lives and blame our father. We
  adopt an "I'll show this bastard what effect he's
  had on me" attitude. We try to punish our father by
  hurting ourself. This is the adult version of the
  child holding his breath or hitting himself in front
  of Dad. In both cases, the message to the father is
  the same: "I'm angry with you. By hurting myself,
  I hope to hurt you." We keep our father a hostage
  by going in and out of jobs, financial crises, jail,
  hospitals, and relationships.

- We blame his failure on his job, health, personality, wife, or upbringing. In this hostage drama we
  cast our father as the victim of circumstances
  beyond his control. We perpetually let him off the
  hook, telling ourself that he is not responsible for
  his behavior. Everyone is "sticking it to him." If it
  is not his boss who is overworking him, then it is
  those terrible back problems which exempt him
  from responsibility. When all else fails, we fall
  back on hardships (the Great Depression, whatever) in his childhood to excuse him. In all these
  cases, the father is cut off and insulated from the
  reality of other people's feelings in what amounts
  to a family conspiracy.

- We push Dad's guilt button. In this hostage posture
  we play upon our father's "good nature" and his
  readily available sense of guilt. Dad feels overly
  responsible for the feelings of the family members.
  He is always overcompensating, overprotecting,

and overindulging them. After all, this is his *job*. The son who holds his father hostage in this drama bleeds dear old Dad of his money and takes advantage of his lack of assertiveness in the family. Dad ends up the family buffoon. He is never taken seriously.

- We hold Dad hostage to Mother's bitterness. We see him through her eyes. And this can provide a dangerous distortion, especially if there has been a divorce. We can easily end up with what the poet Robert Bly has called "a wounded image of our father," caused less by his actions than by our mother's perception of those actions. We internalize her dissatisfactions: "Your father spends too much time in the office." "Your father doesn't really love me." Her complaints become our complaints. Randy, 37, a high school science teacher, discovered that most of his dissatisfaction with his father was actually his mother's: "My parents were divorced when I was seven. My mother was always telling me what a selfish and dishonest man my father was. That went on for years. Whenever I was with my father, I found myself looking for dishonest things he might do, almost like I was trying to catch him at something bad."

In the "hostage" game we pretend that life will go on forever. We are determined to punish or ignore Dad for all time. Or perhaps there is a life-threatening illness or some loss of physical abilities. Then we start to feel the terror of never getting to know our father. We awaken to the fact that he is going to die someday and we have no control over it.

Recently, I was conducting my Alive and Male seminar in Oregon. As each man entered the room, I asked him to write his first name on his tag and his father's first name in the lower righthand corner. No sooner had all thirty-nine of us settled into our circle of chairs than a tall, burly man in his mid-thirties suddenly walked to the center of the room and spoke. "I don't know if . . ." His voice cracked. He fought back the tears. Determined to say what he had come to say, he continued. "I don't know if I'll make it through the day with you guys. I want to. But, you see, my dad died last night."

The man, whose name tag read "Ralph Jr., son of Ralph Sr.," wept in the center of the room. In an instant he found himself surrounded by a small group of men, all perfect strangers. They consoled him and eased his large frame down into the arms of an older man, where he rested.

The group sat in silence until Ralph Jr. spoke again. "We weren't close when I was a boy, but these last few months we had just begun to get through to each other. Oh, God, but I'm going to miss him."

Ralph Jr. had learned too late that secretly blaming our father gets us nowhere. The wishful child in all of us may still believe that had our father been all that we wanted him to be, we would today be a different, better, and happier human being. We ignore the unique strengths which developed in us from being our father's son and blame our father as an excuse for not getting on with the business of our own life. We postpone the realization that it is up to us to make life work. No matter how well intentioned our parents might have been, there is simply no way they could have prepared us for all of life's many experiences and challenges. Life must be lived to be learned.

Reconciliation with Father goes beyond the personal.

We must accept a world in which children are children, adults are adults, and imperfections in parent-child relationships are a given.

Broad-based indictments of our father also fail to consider two other essential factors: our father's identity as a unique individual and the family roles men had during the earlier part of this century.

Understanding our dad as a person, separate and apart from his parental role, reveals his human side. Our father's behavior takes on new meaning in light of his life experiences and circumstances and less as a direct expression of his feelings toward us personally.

Reconciliation with Father goes beyond the personal in yet another way. We must recognize that most of our fathers were taught to "farm out" responsibility for child rearing to Mother while they provided for the family. Rarely did fathering a child mean parenting a child. Our fathers were not taught to relate to their children emotionally. And most of them did not.

Fathers and sons must, therefore, work together for the relationship they want. It is critical to differentiate between our actual father and the father in us when it comes time to clarify our feelings. A story told by John, the older man in whose arms Ralph Jr. had cried earlier that day in my Oregon seminar, illustrates the importance of making that distinction.

"Many years ago I told my father exactly how I felt when he left when I was ten years old. 'I hated you so much,' I said to him. Suddenly, he was my baby and I was holding him. He was crying. I felt like an ass. I felt like I hadn't accomplished a damn thing. What I learned from that experience was that *really* knowing what I felt and being willing to say it was all that counted. Whether my

dad was there didn't mean beans. I had hurt him unneces-
sarily. It was my coming to the point of understanding what
I had to communicate to my father and being strong
enough to say it that mattered. I could have just as easily
dumped my feelings in the forest."

MAN TO MAN

Once again, we can learn from the stories of men who
have risked meeting their fathers halfway and enriched
their lives through a reconciliation.

"My father lives nearby in a motel. He just came out
of a rehabilitation program for alcoholics. Dad had a
serious problem for more than ten years. But he has
got it licked now. Our relationship today is quite
close. But there were times in the past when I hated
him for being a damn drunk and so unstable and irre-
sponsible toward his family. I feel now as though I
have made a journey through hatred to love. Dad has
become very human. He is much more open with
people now. We have discovered all sorts of new
things about each other."

Don, 28, a construction worker in Phoenix

"One day as an adult, I realized that more than
anything I wanted to hug and be hugged by my father. 'Damn it,' I told myself. 'Do it!' So I hopped
into my car and drove 175 miles to see him. Instead
of shaking hands, I just went up to him, put my arms
around him, and gave him a big hug. 'Dad, I love
you,' I told him. And he hugged me back. We were

like two gladiators, just hugging one another as though neither of us ever wanted to stop. It was a wonderful experience and really changed our relationship for the better."

                    Jack, 34, a jazz pianist in Indianapolis

"In the past year I opened a dialogue with my father. I finally got to the point where I could tell him, 'Listen, Dad, I resented you all my life. But I am ready to let all that go. I now understand that you never learned to get close to any of your children. I am letting go of all those bad feelings. Let's give each other a fresh chance and see what comes from it.' He didn't say anything at the time. But then a few days later I got a letter from him. It was very touching."

                        Jack, 39, a geologist in Denver

"My father left when I was one year old. I did not have him in my life again until thirty-five years later when he found me. Until then, the only sense I had of him was through my mother. She hated him. I had learned to hate him, too. After all, he had abandoned me and contributed nothing to my growing up. And then suddenly one evening the phone rang. The voice at the other end said, 'Hi, this is your father. I just flew into town and am at the airport. Can we get together?' I was flabbergasted. He was here for a week. I could never duplicate that experience. My dad gave me back a part of myself that had been lacking. He gave me a way to make peace with my past. I began to see my life in an entirely different light. I suddenly saw how my mother had been cold

to my father and why he had left her. I began to
appreciate myself for having survived a rough beginning. Dad died a few months after our week together.
I so wished we had had more time together."

Stephen, 36, an insurance adjuster in Sacramento

"Long deathwatch with my father. Nothing in his
wasted and lovable life has ever become him so
much as when he moved close to death. It is aston-
ishing to understand that one's father is a brave man:
very brave. The only thing he worried about was my
seeing him in that condition. He cannot ever understand how much better he looked with his arms full
of tubes, with one of those plastic hospital things in
his nose, and the rest of it, than at any time I have
ever seen him before. He was a man up against the
absolute limit. He was giving as well as he got. And
he was afraid of nothing in this world or out of it.
God bless that man. No matter how I came from
him, I hope that it was in joy. For the end is courage."

James Dickey, novelist, *Journals*

EXERCISE NO. 8

Go the nearest large public library and read a newspaper
from the day on which your father was born. (Or an issue
of *Time* or *Newsweek* magazine for that week, if he was
born after 1932.) Imagine the world as it was then and how
different it was from the one you experienced when you
were growing up. (The advertisements are a great help
here.) Ask your father, or men his age if he is now dead,
what it meant to be a man in those times.

EXERCISE NO. 9

Essentially, people hold on to grudges to protect themselves from their own hurt feelings. If they have been badly pained by something their father said or did, then they issue protective warnings to "watch out for Dad." Each time he comes around, their internal alarm sounds.

This exercise will help you get rid of your grudges against your father, all those things that he may have done over the years for which you have never forgiven him.

Take an inventory of all your grudges against your father. You must first admit that you are angry and that your feelings were hurt. Include in the list those things for which you let your father off the hook but never really forgave him.

1. _____

2. _____

3. _____

4. _____

5. _____

Now consider each item one at a time. Ask yourself the following questions:

1. "Have I made a decision about whether to effect a reconciliation on this item?"
2. "If yes, what have I decided? Am I willing to effect a reconciliation or have I determined not to do so at this time?"

3. "Is this reconciliation within myself, or does it also include my father as a participant?"

After sorting through your responses to each of the above items, you should have enough information to identify your terms for a reconciliation. Be specific! "What, if anything, could my father do now to make up for the past? Would a lengthy explanation and apology be sufficient? Or an admission of wrongdoing? Perhaps there is some action Father could undertake now to undo a past mistake?" Before implementing any of these terms, you will want to ask yourself and at least one trusted confidant who knows of your relationship with your father, "Are my terms for reconciliation reasonable?"

EXERCISE NO. 10

Take a trip through the past with your father. Put aside a few hours in the day, take out the family picture albums, and recall some pleasant memories with one another. This exercise is often helpful in those relationships in which the father and son have grown distant over the years. You need to remind yourself that things in the past were not always as bad as you may think they were. So, as the song says, "let the good times roll."

EXERCISE NO. 11

Invite your father on a weekend retreat, just the two of you. Your treat. Select a place, preferably out of town where there will be few distractions. In other words, a rustic lodge in the woods by a lake is a much better setting for this exercise than a hotel in downtown Las Vegas. (You might consider returning to some place where you vacationed as a boy that holds special meaning for you.) Spend the time together, sharing your feelings about one another and your lives. Do some fun things, such as fishing, playing tennis, taking walks together. Keep a journal of your feelings, thoughts, and experiences. Record what your father told you and what you told him.

EXERCISE NO. 12

Write your father a letter for Father's Day. Make it simple and straightforward. Write from your heart. Focus on the positive. Tell him how you feel about him. Give him acknowledgment and appreciation for those things he did right in your relationship over the years. Think of the letter as a gift to your father. Get a mental picture of your father receiving your letter. Imagine him opening, reading, and enjoying it, perhaps proudly sharing the letter with your mother or a close friend.

RECONCILING WITH A DEAD FATHER

A man who has lost his father through death when he was young will often find himself, as an adult, yearning for a tangible contact with him. For men in this predicament their fathers hardly exist except as shadows and ghosts. But dead fathers can be recovered.

John-Henry, a freelance writer from Berkeley, did exactly that. His parents had divorced when he was four. His father moved to another city and died six years later. A conspiracy of silence toward the father settled over the

house as John-Henry grew through boyhood. If he or his
younger brother asked their mother about his father, she cut
the discussion off with the comment: "Your dad drank too
much." His aunts and uncles were equally reticent whenever he approached them for information.

Finally, at 32, John-Henry decided to reconstruct his
father's life and character as best he could. He visited the
house where the family had lived together before the divorce. He located several second cousins on his father's
side of the family, who for the first time shared with him
their memories of the kind of man he had been. They advised him to check out a half sister, Dorothy, sixteen years
older than John-Henry. But none of them had seen her for
almost thirty years or had the slightest idea where she
lived.

"I made a decision then to fly to San Antonio, where my
father had lived out the last years of his life," John-Henry
recalls today. "I spent two days doing some fancy detective
work on my own. I found his grave in a cemetery outside
the city. I had thought I would break into tears when I
finally stood at his graveside. But that never happened. I
think I told myself he wasn't really there but off somewhere else. So I kept looking. The next day it all paid off.
I located my half sister, Dorothy, who lived two hundred
miles away in Houston. I rang her up. 'Hi, Dorothy,' I
said. 'This is a ghost from your past. This is your brother
John-Henry.'

"The next day I drove to Houston. When my sister
opened the door, I was stunned. She looked just like my
father in the few pictures of him that I had. 'I toilet-trained
you when you were a baby,' she said. I stayed with Dorothy and her husband for five days. We talked nonstop
about Father. She was eighteen when Mom and Dad sepa-

rated, so she had an adult perspective on those events. She gave me a sense of my father I never had before. I learned about his family, who had first come west in 1775 with Daniel Boone, his boyhood in Kentucky, his tough times in medical school, when he had married for the first time, his devotion as a doctor to his patients, the breakup of his marriage to my mother, and the series of strokes that finally killed him. But most of all, my sister told me that Father had loved his two sons and was terribly broken up at having to lose us in the divorce. When I left, she gave me a collection of letters, pictures, and personal effects belonging to Father. I knew I had recovered an important part of myself that had always been missing. For the first time I felt, really felt, I had a father. And I had discovered that he was a good man, one I liked and would be proud to call Dad."

EXERCISE NO. 13

Do a reconstruction of your father. If you have never known your father, this will give you a tangible sense of him that you never had. But this exercise is useful if you did know your father or if he is still alive. It will give you a more balanced perspective on him and help you recognize that there were entire areas of your father's life that were off limits to you.

The following sources may be available to you as you go about the reconstruction:

1. your father, if still alive
2. your mother
3. your father's brothers and sisters

4. your grandparents
5. your father's friends or colleagues at work

Use a tape recorder. Tape conversations in person or over the phone as these people talk about both the positive and the negative aspects of your father. Assemble a portrait of your father as he was, not as he appeared in your judgments. Stay away from asking "why." Look rather at determining the "what" and "how." Some of the things you will want to learn are: What was his youth like? What kind of experiences did he have with his own father? What were his intellectual resources? His emotional resources? What skills did he bring to bear on the task of living? What sort of moral character did he have?

Remember—with patience you *can* put Humpty Dumpty back together again.

A SON'S CREDO

My relationship with my own father has today become one of the most loving and rewarding in my life. I have given up my secrets with and about my father. Here are some things that, as a son, I have had to learn.

- I will not ask my father for anything I am not prepared to give him in return. For example, I will not ask my father to be open and vulnerable with me when I am unwilling to be the same with him.

- I will accept my father for who he is as a person, including his weaknesses and limits as well as his strengths.

- I will stop competing with my father, either by being like him or by being "different and better."

- I will not undermine my own accomplishments and value by constantly comparing myself with my father.

- I will remember that I'm no angel. I have not always been reasonable or fair with my father.

- I will let go of all the unrealistic expectations that I may have for my father.

- I will stop trying to change my father.

- I will look for the good and positive in my father.

- I will get myself out of my father's relationship with my mother.

- I will be specific in my requests of my father, always respecting his right to say no.

- I will understand the era from which my father came, in contrast with the era in which I grew up.

- I will take responsibility for my relationship with my father, stating specifically what I want to give as well as receive.

Father's Day will come and go this year, as it does every year, with lost opportunities for reconciliation with Father. Sons and daughters will scramble in department stores for their "personalized" gifts amidst the electric shavers, neckties, and easy chairs. Ad slogans will compete for "the best gift you can give."

Don't be fooled.

There are no better gifts for Father's Day than our love and another chance for reconciliation.

Can we afford to let that opportunity pass once more?

Chapter FOUR

Man to Man: Why a Good Friend Is Hard to Find

MALE FRIENDSHIPS AS SECOND-CLASS RELATIONSHIPS

"Sure I got buddies," a California politician once confessed to writer Phyllis Chesler. "Lots of buddies. And we couldn't get too much done without coming through for each other. But they're not my friends. You can't afford friends when you want to get things done. Power isn't kept by a system of friendship. It's kept by how fast you can move with a change of time or need, how well organized your people are, how easily you can drop another guy when he's wrong or going under. The people I relax with are in other areas. But even there, even with my wife's relatives, I gotta do favors, and I keep my ears open, too. I have allies. I have enemies. And I have family. But I have no friends."

In this chapter I want to take up a major problem of

most contemporary men—their failure to establish close friendships with other men, friendships in which they feel secure enough to confide their deepest fears and feelings. The sorry fact is that men today often have no close male friends. This is so common that it is taken for granted and rarely commented upon. Many of the men I counsel admit they do not have one intimate male friend in whom they can place complete trust and confidence. Not that we do not have our tennis, golfing, and drinking "buddies." But in most instances we do not relate to these companions in an emotionally open manner. What we really experience deep inside remains a mystery, even to our "closest" friends.

"Men's relationships with other men, which could be a true echo of their manhood, are generally characterized by thinness, insincerity, and even chronic weariness," writes Professor Stuart Miller in *Men and Friendship.* "Since most men don't let themselves think or feel about friendship, this immense and collective disappointment is usually concealed, sloughed over, or shrugged away."

Look around you at the next party you attend. The chances are that the women will be grouped on one side of the room, talking out their feelings about their jobs, their families, their marriages, and their latest emotional ups and downs. The men will stand together on the other side of the room, discussing the latest sports personality to nail down a multimillion-dollar contract or the fact that they may be due for a promotion at work. It is a safe bet they will *not* be discussing their emotional ups and downs with one another. Sports. Work. A new car. These are safe subjects for most men. But not their fears about growing old. Or feeling trapped. Or feeling lonely. Or feeling scared.

The sad fact is that most men simply do not trust one

another. All too often men together in a room are like tigers entering a caged arena—wary, silently fearful, distrustful, perpetually guarded. Most men recognize this. But they are quick to defend themselves. "You have to protect yourself," an assistant bank manager once advised me. "If you show your cards to other men, they may use that information against you."

Most men do form bonds with other men when they are "thrown together" at certain points in life, such as their years in the military or at college. At these times their needs for companionship and belonging are no longer met by familiar home and family surroundings, and they are less restricted by class and ethnic boundaries. The pressures of establishing a home, family, and career have yet to make themselves felt.

But in time we leave the military and graduate from college. Our world then starts to narrow. At this time friendship ceases to be an issue of concern with most men. A majority of married men say goodbye to their close buddies at their bachelor parties. When we marry, we cease spending much time or energy nurturing and developing close friendships with other men. We focus our attention instead on our wives, our families, and the "contacts" we make at work. Friendships take a back seat. Those relationships with a concrete function and purpose in our lives are allowed to take precedence, even over the youthful friendship bonds we formed many years before.

THE FRIENDSHIP RUT

As creatures of habit, we all get into the friendship rut. We hang around the same three drinking buddies year after year, boring ourselves with the same small talk. Or we make the Wednesday-night poker game "with the guys," just as we have done every Wednesday night for the past ten years. Keeping the familiar routine is much easier than making changes in our lives. We resign ourselves to the way things are and always have been. We avoid taking risks. And, predictably, we get from our investment what we put into it. Very little. Then we tell ourselves, "Why should I invest time and energy into something that provides so little in return?"

Many men have come to view the need for a friend as a bit of an embarrassment, a throwback to adolescence. Most of us will admit that in our youth we enjoyed the friendship of close buddies. We remember fondly the good times we had with them in high school, at college, and in the service. But something happened to us along the way. We became men. And "being a man" means the same as being "all grown up." We set about to secure our status as self-sufficient adults, functioning in a male hierarchy based on money, status, and power. No longer did we prize the intrinsic worth of one friend to another. We settled for a few good "buddies" whom we never really got to know and who never got to know us.

And we subscribed to the "Six Don'ts of Male Friendship":

1. Don't let your guard down (except after a few drinks).
2. Don't show too much emotion (unless it's anger).
3. Don't become too involved, friendly, or frivolous.
4. Don't let on how much you really care.
5. Don't touch one another (except after scoring a basket or making a touchdown).

6. Don't act like a sissy or appear feminine in any
   way.

BEER BUDDIES: THE SYMBOL OF FRIENDSHIP FOR THE AMERICAN MAN

Short of having sex together, two men may do just about anything as long as there is beer present. Beer has done more to bring men together over the ages than baseball, football, and the Indy 500 combined. "Let's go for a beer" is male code for "Let's spend some time together." And don't the beer companies know it! Tens of millions of dollars are spent each year on television and print advertisements that portray men gathered together to drink beer, whether it is after work, at sports, or on an outdoor adventure. Beer drinking, the ads tell us, is the way to become "one of the boys."

Beer and masculinity go hand in hand. Today, more than ever before, beer is tied into men's friendships and reward systems. Beer not only provides a reason for two men to sit together without public suspicion. It also furnishes us with a safe means for letting our guard down, opening up, and showing some emotions. We can be sentimental, tearful, silly, and affectionate with other men—*if* we have been drinking beer. And later if we are embarrassed by our actions, then we can always claim that we had "one too many" and none of our buddies will think the worse of us. The advertising agencies for the big breweries understand this. That is why they script their television commercials to tap into the unspoken needs of millions of men for man-to-man companionship.

The secret men burden themselves with in this area is

that we really are hungry for friendship with other men at the same time we deny its importance in our own lives. We will not allow ourselves to get together with male friends because we enjoy their company. It is not "safe" simply to want some male companionship. We have to legitimize the feeling. We have to throw in a card game, a ball game, or some beer to make the occasion a "safe" one.

Sports has freed men to play, cheer, and express their feelings in one another's presence. But it has also created a nation of sports widows among wives and women friends. Beer has, likewise, brought a great many men together outside the competitive world of work. But it has contributed to the nation's number one health problem, alcoholism.

Men do not need beer, hard liquor, or recreational drugs in order to exist. But we do need human companionship. Even the most staunchly self-reliant among us sometimes needs a friend. Stepping outside the "beer buddy" syndrome can prove the first step to satisfying these companion needs.

EXERCISE NO. 1

Here are several exercises that will allow you to take an honest inventory of your friends. List below all those people you care about the most and who care about you.

My Friends

1. _____   2. _____

3. _____   4. _____

5. _____   6. _____

7. _____   8. _____

9. _____   10. _____

In the above list of friends, how many of them are men? _____ How many are women? _____

EXERCISE NO. 2

Usually, when I ask men to list their male friends, they give me the names of friends from their past—buddies from their youth, fraternity brothers in college, or guys they knew when they were in the armed forces. These long-distance friends actually turn out to be men they see only on special occasions once every year or so. The active time of the friendship occurred years before but the bond lingers on.

Then I ask these men to check the names of men on their list who rank as *active* friends, friends they have now and see on a regular basis. Frequently, none of the names will be checked. We tend to see who our friends were, not who they are today, because many of us would end up having to admit to ourselves that we have so few men's names we could list in the "active friends" category.

Below I want you to take an inventory of your male friends. In the column on the left list your "inactive" friends from the past. Use the column on the right to list your "active" friends, those men who are a part of your life today, the individuals you can become actively involved with on a day-to-day, week-to-week basis.

Past Friends (relatively inactive)	**Friends Today** (active)
1. _____	1. _____
2. _____	2. _____
3. _____	3. _____
4. _____	4. _____
5. _____	5. _____

EXERCISE NO. 3

Let's look more closely at the activities you share with your men friends. What do you do when you get together with your buddies? Check off the most common activities you engage in with your male friends.

1. _____ play sports
2. _____ go camping
3. _____ see a movie
4. _____ hustle women
5. _____ eat out at a restaurant
6. _____ play chess, backgammon, poker, or another game
7. _____ simply spend time together, discussing your lives
8. _____ attend a party
9. _____ bring your families together in shared activities

10. _____ go out drinking
11. _____ work
12. _____ other _____
13. _____   _____
14. _____   _____

Look over the list of activities that you checked above.
Ask yourself whether or not they allow you and your male
friends the opportunity to share each other's lives and feelings at a more intimate level. Or are you so engaged in
activities that relatively little chance exists for you and one
or two friends to enter into a frank exchange of the highs
and lows of your lives?

THE WALLS WE HIDE BEHIND

When a man enters a crowded room, it is as automatic
for him to look past the other men there as it is for him to
size up quickly all the women. Most men know exactly
what they want in a woman. We are quick to pay them
compliments on a great figure, a stylish dress, a nice smile,
a clever sense of humor. We have thought long and hard
about what pleases us in a woman.

But just the opposite happens when we are with other
men. Most men would be hard put to define precisely what
they like and do not like in other men. It is something to
which we rarely give much thought. Furthermore, we are
reluctant to pay other men compliments. Rarely do we risk
telling another man how much we value his personal qualities. We hesitate to put our true feelings on the line and act
disappointed because these friendships never seem to
deepen.

"Good fences make good neighbors," a farmer in a Robert Frost poem insists. Many men would agree. All too often we play it safe and erect walls between ourselves and other men. Behind these walls we hide our secrets, fears, and insecurities. Here are four of the most common barriers.

The Wall of Competition

Two men meet and introduce themselves. Almost immediately each one asks himself, "How much better or less a man am I than he?" Evaluating oneself in constant comparisons with other men is a major characteristic of men who throw up the Wall of Competition between themselves and other men. The bricks in this wall may be made from money, job titles, or status symbols such as cars, attractive women, and designer clothing. Such value comparisons of our own and other men's "worth" block our ability to see and appreciate what is unique in each of us. Men whose self-esteem is fragile frequently revert to this wall to prove their worth over and over again.

The Wall of Women

Some men use the women in their lives, including their wives, girlfriends, mothers, and secretaries, as buffers between themselves and other men. For some men, this is a throwback to their childhood when Mom was always there to act as an intermediary between them and their fathers. For others, it is a way to compensate for the lack of basic social skills or for shyness. Such men lack the necessary assertiveness and fall back upon women to represent them. Such men often enroll women to keep the conversation going and set a general non-competitive tone in which they can relate safely to other men. Men who experience discomfort or feel threatened when dealing with other men often come to depend upon women as go-betweens, peacemakers, and mediators. "We'll have to get our husbands together" is the often-heard statement of women who recognize that, alone, these men would remain walled off from one another.

The Wall of Fear

Men's fear of rejection and judgment at the hands of other men constitutes another major wall. We are more sensitive to what other men think than many of us let on. The Wall of Fear is well guarded. We keep our insecurities at work a secret from our male colleagues for fear they may use that information against us. And we worry that our best buddy may start stalking "our" woman if we tell him our fear that she may be falling out of love with us. Above all, we worry that other men will judge us as "less a man" if they learn that behind our carefully crafted exterior we are sometimes depressed, scared, and uncertain.

The Wall of Fear also stands between us men in another important way. Many men fear that if they get too close to another man physically or emotionally, others then will perceive them as "gay." It is an unfortunate aspect of our culture that the American man's preoccupation with losing his "maleness" can often preclude the kind of healthy close male comraderie that exists in other cultures. Close male friends in many Mediterranean countries, for example, often show their friendship with lots of touching—slaps on the back, line dances, and warm hugs—all without fear that their masculinity will be compromised. In our country we allow back-slapping and butt-slapping only on the playing fields, where there can be no possibility of misinterpreting healthy heterosexual male closeness for homosexuality. And American men are the poorer for it.

The Wall of Ignorance

The Wall of Ignorance is perhaps the saddest of them all. Because we never allow ourselves an opportunity to get to know other men in ways that permit a mutual exchange of feelings, we never understand the ways in which men are truly different from as well as similar to us. We content ourselves with the surfaces and never see the realities beneath. Distance breeds ignorance. And ignorance in turn breeds prejudice. It is much easier to harbor prejudices against other men when we insist upon judging them from afar. We allow what we do not know about other men— our ignorance—to stand as a barrier rather than reaching out to understand one another better.

How many of these walls against other men have you erected in your life?

THE BENEFITS OF MAN-TO-MAN FRIENDSHIPS

Most men feel more comfortable drawing their closest friends from women rather than other men. We fall back on our wives, lovers, mothers, sisters, and daughters. We decide early on that women make better friends. Many men know from experience that women are generally better listeners than other men. They are more understanding, less competitive, and less judgmental. Men feel safer talking to a woman about their fears and uncertainties than to another man. We perceive women as more loving and trustworthy than other men.

"So who needs other men?" we tell ourselves. "Why take a chance?" Most of us don't. And on those rare occasions when we do risk opening up with another man, more often than not we are disappointed with the response. Male friendships have proven a discouraging investment for many men. And yet today we know more about why this has occurred than ever before. Consequently, we are in a better position to reverse this trend and enjoy satisfying friendships with other men.

Any man who has ever had a "real friend" knows the power of friendship to enrich our lives. Having a male friend empowers us in several important ways.

We Validate Our Experiences as a Man

Once we open our world to another man, we learn that we are not alone in our fears, insecurities, uncertainties, and desires. Nothing is "wrong" with us, as we might have secretly suspected. Through a friendship with another man, we affirm much that is good and strong in us as men. Frank and honest exchanges of experiences allow us to gain a fresh and clear perspective on ourselves.

We Lessen Our Dependencies on Women

Taught that only women can help us satisfy our emotional needs in relationships, we have disqualified other men as intimate companions. We go in quest of female companionship and turn our backs on other men. We grow closer and more dependent on women, neglecting friendships with men, thus creating an imbalance in our lives. We end up emotionally lopsided, relating only to women. And then we start demanding that our women act more like "one of the boys." When what we really want is interaction with males, we should get together with other men. Instead we fall into the trap of the popular song and ask, "Why can't a woman be more like a man?" Friendships with other men put a balance back into our lives and strengthen our marriages because there is less emotional clinging to the women in our lives.

We Develop Our Skills at Intimacy

Men who achieve intimacy with other men enjoy a sense of acceptance by their peers. We become more certain of who we are. We develop more self-esteem. This provides a strong foundation from which we can build relationships with others. Having established ourselves as a man among men, we build confidence and free ourselves to trust others in close relationships.

Male Friends Help Us in Times of Crises with Women

The additional value of close male friends became apparent to a man in one of my groups after his recent separation from his wife. "Since our separation, I've reestablished friendships with men I had known over the years, relationships I had neglected when I was married," he told us one evening. "It has been the one positive thing to come out of this mess. I've got my friends back. I was forced to reach out and ask for their friendship now that I no longer have my wife to fall back upon. And thank God for my men friends, because I am not ready to start relating socially to women again for some time."

Friends Protect Us Against Life's Stresses

Modern medical research confirms the truth in the Beatles' song: We really do get by with a little help from our friends. Studies have shown that men with at least one close friend in whom they could confide about themselves and their problems had, in effect, a buffer against such crises as the loss of a wife or job, a chronic illness, and the psychological stresses of aging. In terms of their morale and health, these men have a significant edge over men who lack a close confidant.

Friends Minimize Loneliness

Feelings of loneliness are lessened when we have friends. We can create new families of friends to replace those we have lost or who live thousands of miles away. And good social supports help us balance needs which might otherwise yield an overdependence upon our wives and families.

Our Male Friends Become Valuable Resources

A tight circle of male friends also provides a host of additional benefits: support in times of emergency, companions to share good times and fun in our leisure hours, a source of information, money, and professional expertise in areas other than our own. For years men have looked enviously upon women's formal and informal support groups and networks. Men who have developed close personal bonds and trust with a range of other men are free to support one another in a variety of endeavors. Personal and professional networking, through friendships, often opens the doors to an even wider range of contacts and possibilities. Competition gives way to cooperation.

Friends Reaffirm Our Sense of Being Alive

And, finally, friends help us experience what it means to be alive. Too many men today rely upon activities to do that for them, taking up everything from hang-gliding to chasing after women to give them the rush of energy they identify with "being alive." But neither diversion nor the accumulation of wealth gives us a true sense of life. We experience that richness only through intimate relationships with others. "Just recall the great feeling of physical energy you get when you meet a new friend," writes Eugene Kennedy, a psychologist at Loyola University in Chicago. "It is one of the natural highs of life to discover that there is a human being who responds to me and I to him. Friendship breaks through a person's shell so that he can taste and experience life more fully."

MAN TO MAN

Men are adept at talking about things rather than what they feel about those things. Our willingness to be emotionally honest and vulnerable can make the difference between an acquaintanceship and a friendship. Once again, we can see ourselves in other men's stories of their lives.

"Just once, I'd like my friend Steve to ask me something personal. He seems more interested in discussing business and sports. I tried to open him up once by sharing something from my own life when he told me he was struggling in his marriage. But he told me everything was all right. You gotta watch those guys who always tell you everything is 'all right.' Half the time they're lying."

Mike, 36,
an appliance salesman from San Jose

"Now that I think about it, even with my closest male friends there's a nervousness sometimes when we talk to one another. It's like we never found that middle ground between being boys and being men."

John, 29, an auto mechanic in Baltimore

"All my friends are women. I'm beginning to feel like one of the girls!"

Carl, 52, a high school teacher in St. Louis

"Bob is my closest male friend. Last year his wife died suddenly of cancer. It was a pretty traumatic time for the both of us. I flew to Chicago to be with him. There was too much going on then to get deep into our relationship. Afterwards I realized that we had been open with one another but only to a point. Past that point, we would clam up, as men tend to do. Several months later my wife left me. Bob took advantage of a long weekend to fly in for a visit. He and I went up to a cabin in the mountains. It was just the two of us. There we were, two guys, one who had lost his wife to cancer, the other to divorce. It seemed we had nothing to lose. We spent forty-eight hours just getting to know one another, spilling our guts about our relationships with our fathers, mothers, wives. I learned more about him and he about me in those two days than in twenty years of friendship. What forced it was that we didn't have anything to lose and everything to gain."

Gary, 44, a lawyer from Denver

"I've been going to sales conventions for years, and it's always pretty much the same thing. All the married guys away from their wives for a few days, chasing women when they're not attending meetings.

Don't get me wrong. I like to check out good-looking ladies, too. But I have no interest in taking any of them to bed. I'm a happily married man. Usually, I just go back to my room, call the family, and then fall asleep after watching television. But one night I didn't feel like grabbing a quick bite to eat and going back to my room. Instead I asked a guy I know with the eastern division of our company if he'd join me for dinner. It was one of the most enjoyable dinners I've ever had out. We talked until midnight about our lives and really let our guards down. I made a good friend that night."

> Mark, 39,
> a computer salesman from Los Angeles

"No, I have no male friends. If you get too friendly with a man, people will think you are a queer."

> Andy, 47, a machinist in Cleveland

"Three years ago I discovered who my true friends were when severe back pains put me in bed for two months. I really needed help. Some days I could not sit up or get out of the bed for more than ten minutes at a time. Some of my friends simply dropped out of my life altogether. Others called regularly to ask about my condition. And then there were Bill and Tony. I don't know how I could have made it without them. At least one of them visited me every day. They bought my groceries, ran my errands, did my laundry, and listened patiently to my endless, boring accounts of my progress. They were my links to the outside world. Bill and Tony made me feel valued and gave me some good laughs at a time when physical pain was the overwhelming reality in my life."

John, 34, a carpenter, Boston

"It only takes about thirty seconds for my friend Steve and me to lapse into our traditional gibing session—no matter how long it's been since we've seen each other. He'll enter my apartment, cock his head, squint at my steadily receding hairline, and say, 'Yup, another half inch gone!' I'll look at his steadily advancing paunch and counter, 'You ought to get back into jogging, ol' buddy.'

"Steve is my best friend and has been for years. This exchange of put-downs is our way of showing our affection for each other. Our friendship is often more a battle of wits than an exchange of honest feelings. But these insults actually reassure us more than they assault. As soon as Steve hits me with his favorite hairline gibe and I razz him about his battle with the bulge, we know that all is well between us. And to make sure nobody's feelings are hurt, we've developed the 'Swiss bank.' Just as wealthy people sometimes hide money in Swiss bank accounts to avoid paying taxes, we deposit our insecurities in an imaginary account to avoid the sting of jokes about sensitive topics. For instance, to prevent Steve from comparing my size-fourteen feet to small boats, I say, without further explanation, 'Okay, the feet are in the Swiss bank.' Thus I'm guaranteed that, because of our mutual respect, he'll never bring them up again."

Jake, 41, a freelance writer, New York City

"I used to think Bill and I were good friends. We got together on a regular basis to fish or play golf. We always talked a lot about our lives and values and genuinely liked one another. But things changed when my career took off and his didn't. Then Bill changed from being a friend to being a sniper, and I knew he had not been a true friend."

George, 37,
an accountant, Jacksonville, Florida

"I've always been a loner. I don't have many friends. My job keeps me on the road a lot, so I have a lot of acquaintances in various cites where my business takes me. I am never home long enough to establish friendships there. Oh, there are guys at the office I'm friendly with. We cover for one another when we are late or want to take a long lunch. But if I want to talk my problems out with someone, I'll pick a woman. I meet plenty of those on the road. And they are usually good listeners."

Charlie, 36, a salesman, Dallas

"After my wife gave birth to our second child, I called all the relatives. When it was time to leave, I kissed my wife and new baby goodbye and went to a nearby restaurant where my three best buddies were waiting for me. It was one of those times when I was so full of emotions that I didn't want to be alone. I really felt the guys were with me. It was one of the best evenings I have ever had with my friends."

Barry, 32, a social worker, Detroit

"Jack was my best buddy throughout high school. We were opposites in some ways. I was shy and introverted. Jack was streetwise and a lady's man. When I was 21 and convinced that I would never get laid, it was Jack who took me across the river to a whorehouse to lose my virginity. After college we went our separate ways and lost track of each other. But over the years I often thought about Jack and our good times together. Then one summer when I had returned to the old neighborhood for a couple of days, I ran into his mother on the street. She told me that Jack was a producer with one of the big networks on the West Coast. She gave me his home phone number. Later I took a chance and rang the network and got him on the phone. It was Jack! The next night we got together for dinner. It was just like old times. I see Jack now perhaps once a year, and we call each other every three or four months. The breaks never seem to hurt the relationship. When we are together, we are the best of friends and open up about our most intimate feelings, just like when we were kids. His friendship means a great deal to me."

Tim, 45, a university professor, San Diego

"John and I went back to the fourth grade. We had been the best of friends for over thirty-five years. One morning I awoke abruptly at four o'clock and sat straight up in bed. My mind was filled with John. 'What's wrong?' my wife asked. 'Something has happened to John,' I told her. Later that day John's parents called from Illinois to say he had been killed a few hours earlier in an automobile accident. In a way it was both frightening and strangely comforting because I felt that John had taken the opportunity to say goodbye."

Fred, 46, a family doctor in Memphis

CHOOSING FRIENDS

I have often imagined a computer friendship service for men who are eager to make new friends but have trouble meeting other men who would be good candidates. Men who are full of creative and bright ideas about where they can go and what they can do to meet new women suddenly seem to draw a blank when they decide they need a new male friend in their lives.

Recently, one of my clients, Bud, was quite depressed because he suddenly found himself without close male friends. "I had two close buddies all my life," he told me. "In the last year I lost them both. One died. He was only 43. The other moved to Houston. Suddenly, I didn't have a friend in the world. My wife was wonderful about it. She really understood and tried to help me. It's a terribly lonely feeling." On several occasions Bud tried without much success to make friends with men he had known over the years at his office and in his neighborhood. But nothing seemed to work. "I'm about as easygoing a guy as anybody out there," Bud told me later. "I can get along with just about anybody. But I've gone through hell trying to get closer to some of these guys. It just hasn't worked out very well."

Bud's story illustrates perfectly a lesson that few men understand—the extent to which the capacity for friendship is a genuine social skill, an area of competence that needs to be learned.

FIVE KINDS OF FRIENDS

Over the years I have interviewed hundreds of men about their friendships with other men. From these conversations I learned that men's friendships with other men generally take five different forms. Friendships may progress over time. We may move a friend from one category to another. Or all our friends may fall into just two or three of the various categories.

The Best Friend

The Best Friend is our staunchest supporter. He will stick with us through the best of times and the worst of times. The Best Friend is someone we know intimately. We can share with him our most private thoughts without fear that we will be rejected or compromise the friendship. Therefore, we never feel compelled to conceal anything from him. A Best Friend is not afraid to take risks with us by initiating new activities, expressing his anger or displeasure at something we have done, giving and asking for affection, or opening up with us about what really concerns him in his life. This friendship has usually withstood the pressures of time, distance, and at least one major falling-out.

The Good Buddy

The Good Buddy is a friend and companion we can call on in a time of need. Although his friendship may be important to us, it is not one that encompasses the more intimate dimensions of the Best Friend. But he is available when we need him. A Good Buddy will allow himself to get just so close. He cares for us more than he can readily admit and expresses that affection indirectly through his reliability and availability. And then he draws a line. He is quite reluctant to disclose his true feelings, and so we never get to know him as well as a Best Friend.

The Party Friend

The Party Friend is always available when we want company for a night "on the town with the boys" or an afternoon sporting event. His talk is always superficial, dealing with topics generated by the action of the moment, whether it is a beautiful lady who just walked by or the other team's performance in the volleyball game you just played. The Party Friend likes to share our good times but we would never think of calling upon him for support and consolation during those bad times when we feel depressed, uncertain, and fearful. After a few hours together, we part, saying, "Oh, we have to get together real soon again." But both of us know the friendship will wait until the next party.

The Friend from the Past

The Friend from the Past is one with whom we share a history that may go back to our childhood. He may have been our buddy in the house next door when we were in fifth grade, a tent mate at summer camp, a member of the same high school football team, a fraternity brother at college, or a fellow soldier. The Friend from the Past is a peg on which we hang a bag of good memories and recollections. When we get together with a Friend from the Past, we slip into the old roles, tell the old stories, and recall the old times. It becomes a nostalgia trip in honor of earlier times we shared and those memories we still treasure. Friends from the past are like living snapshot albums of our history and usually have very little to do with our lives in the present.

The Institutional Friend

Friendships made and kept by association at work or through a church or civic organization usually never grow beyond the level of "institutional brotherhood." The Institutional Friend relates to us in a set, predictable fashion along the lines established by the organization. Little is risked and little gained besides a sense of belonging to a particular group. Occasionally, some men will use institutional brotherhood as a platform to develop lasting and meaningful friendships with other men. But for the most part the Institutional Friend plays it safe and prefers to keep the friendship within predictable boundaries.

EXERCISE NO. 4

Let's take an additional assessment of your friends in light of the above categories.

My Best Friends are: 1. _____
                              2. _____
                              3. _____
                              4. _____

My Good Buddies are: 1. _____
                              2. _____
                              3. _____
                              4. _____

My Party Friends are: 1. _____
                               2. _____
                               3. _____
                               4. _____

My Friends from the Past are: 1. _____
                               2. _____
                               3. _____
                               4. _____

My Institutional Friends are: 1. _____
                               2. _____
                               3. _____
                               4. _____

I talked before about friendship ruts. Until we discover what is missing and what we want in our friendships, it is almost impossible to break out of a friendship rut.

EXERCISE NO. 5

Look over your lists from Exercise No. 4. If you have no Best Friends or only one or two and lots of Good Buddies, Party Friends, Friends from the Past, and Institutional Friends, then perhaps you may want to start thinking about working harder on certain friendships in an effort to improve their quality.

A first step in this direction is to make an inventory of those qualities you like in a friend. Next to each item on the list below put the initials of a male friend not currently a best friend whose company is most rewarding for that particular quality.

1. I get to learn and explore with _____.
2. I get to play, be silly, and spontaneous with _____.
3. I get to play competitively with _____.
4. I receive affection and nurturance from _____.
5. I feel risky and adventuresome with _____.
6. I am most happy with _____.
7. I have my guard down the most when I am with _____.
8. I share my feelings of disappointment, uncertainty, and fear with _____.
9. I'm at my best with _____.
10. I open up about myself most easily with _____.
11. I feel most relaxed when I am with _____.
12. I like who I am the most when I am with _____.

EXERCISE NO. 6

On the basis of the last two exercises, list below three men you know who you think are the best candidates for promotion to the status of Best Friends.

1. _____

2. _____

3. _____

MY FRIENDSHIP WITH TERRY

We frequently make the same mistake with our friends that we do with our fathers. We fail to acknowledge how much we love and appreciate them. And then frequently it is too late. We lose them without ever having told them how much their friendship has meant to us.

Terry has been the most important friend of my adult life. We go back a long way. It has been years since Terry and I spent hours on the tennis court, exerting ourselves to win a point and then collapsing in laughter over a witty remark. And I still think of him when I put on the climbing boots I wore when we climbed Mount Blanca one summer day almost a decade ago. And then there was his divorce from his first wife, Joycelyn, when a piece of my world fell apart as well

Our paths diverged, and we each took our families to different parts of the country. I moved to southern California while Terry set out to build his dream home in Oregon We were both busy setting up new careers. The phone calls and letters slowly slackened off. Our friendship, so intense only a few years before, became dormant. Then I decided to visit Terry in Oregon. Our friendship reawakened. Our reunion reaffirmed the loving feelings which, although they had been unexpressed for many years, had never left us. From that point on, Terry and I were in touch with each other on a regular basis. We began to recognize the different directions our lives had taken. And we were slowly making our way back into each other's life.

A phone call last year abruptly changed all that. It was Terry. And I could tell from the tone of his voice something was wrong. "Ken, there's something I have to tell you," he

said. "Last week my doctor found a cancer in my colon. I
go into the hospital in five days for surgery. Now, I don't
want you getting all worked up about this. I'm going to be
all right."

Several days went by before I could really accept the
fact that my best friend had cancer. This was no story I was
reading in the newspaper about a stranger on the other side
of the country. This was my Terry, who was just 36 years
old and had three great kids, a beautiful new wife, and
everything to live for.

A few hours after the operation, Terry's wife, Susan,
called with the news. "Oh, Ken, the doctors had him in the
operating room for over five hours," she sobbed. "They
found more cancer in his liver. They give him only six to
nine months to live. How can I tell Terry?"

Three days later, I was on a plane heading up the Pacific
coast toward Ashland, Oregon, and a very sick Terry. I
spent the entire trip playing back in my mind the history of
our friendship. I remembered our first meeting when his
tall, athletic appearance, topped off by a red beard and
warm smile, drew my immediate attention. We quickly
warmed to one another. I was the new kid on the block,
having just started work at the community mental health
center in a small Colorado town. Terry worked there, too.

Soon afterwards Terry and I were among those selected
for a six-day workshop on group psychotherapy that was
held in a beautiful mountain retreat in the Colorado
Rockies. We drove up together and shared a room. We
were together for most of our leisure time. We had so much
in common. And yet we each felt there was much we could
learn from the other. Terry was open with me in a way no
man had ever been before. He was not afraid to trust me
with his most intimate feelings. I felt such a relief to share

with him some of my own secrets, things I had never thought of sharing with any man before. This was the beginning of the closest friendship I have ever known.

Our families became close. Terry was there in the hospital with me when Jenna, our first daughter, was born. I fell into his arms as I came out of the delivery room. I stayed there in his arms, crying the tears of a new father, tears of joy, fear, and exhaustion. And it was from watching Terry with his two sons, Shane and Kelsey, that I learned how to combine those right amounts of firmness and playfulness when dealing with my kids.

All these memories flashed through my mind on that plane to Ashland. Late that afternoon I stood beside Terry's bed in the hospital. "Damn you, Terry, you'll do anything to get me up here," I joked with him. The surgery had devastated him. But Terry did his best to reassure me that he would soon be all right.

I spent the next week with my friend. Sometimes we sat together in long silences in his hospital room. I held his hand while he slept or hugged him when he cried. I was there for one purpose only, to be with my friend. We talked about his dying, about the difficult decisions that lay ahead, about the search for alternative treatments, and about his anger with himself for getting the cancer. There were harsh financial realities that had to be faced. Terry's medical expenses mounted daily. I assured him that his friends would help out and that his only job was to recuperate from the surgery.

Before I returned to San Diego, I resolved to give an Alive and Male seminar in the Ashland area and donate the proceeds to Terry. A group of Terry's friends agreed to handle the logistics and publicize the seminar. The following month when I returned to Ashland, the entire community had joined us to raise money for Terry. Across the state, newspapers, radio talk shows, and television news departments gave the story a big play. The seminar proved to be one of the most joyful I have ever conducted. Terry was there. And at the end of the second day, it was clear to all of us that the entire community had opened its heart. As one man there said, "This experience has produced a ripple that will become a wave in our community." Terry died on May 31, 1985, the day after his thirty-eighth birthday. He fought valiantly and surrendered his life as unselfishly as he had lived it. Because of our willingness to open up, Terry and I enjoyed a richness few men ever come to experience.

HOLDING BACK

What are the ways we men hold ourselves back from deeper and more meaningful friendships? *We make excuses!* Below I have listed some of the most common excuses we use. How many of them are in your repertoire?

"I called him last time. It's his turn now!"

How many times have we used this excuse not to initiate contact? We act as though taking turns is the only way to ensure equality in a friendship.

"If he really cared about the friendship, he would have called me by now."

This is a variation on the first excuse and just as feeble. Insisting that a friend does not care because he has not called is, more often than not, an erroneous assumption.

"My wife won't let me."

We pass the responsibilities on to our wives and blame them for our failure to get together. We play the role of the henpecked husband and use our wives to make excuses: "I would love to get together for dinner with you tonight, Fred, but Vicki wants me home tonight."

"I don't have the time."

This is the favorite excuse of the man who uses perpetual busyness to avoid intimacy with his friends. "I just can't take the time away from my job or the family" is another variation on this excuse.

"Jack owns his own company. Why would a man like that be interested in being friends with a mere salesman like me?"

There are hundreds of variations on this excuse. "Married men don't get along well with single men." Or: "I've seen the way Bob is on the golf course, and I don't think I could ever be friends with him." All these excuses have one thing in common. They embody prejudices we employ to dismiss or disqualify ourselves and other men from serious contention as friends and companions.

"How can I be friends after what that bastard did to me?"

We hold grudges. We give up important friendships, often over single incidents. We get angry with a friend who has hurt us. Instead of talking the matter over with him in an attempt to resolve the difficulty, we simply terminate the friendship and shut our former friend out of our lives forever.

EXERCISE NO. 7

Men too often play it safe with their male friends by putting large areas of their personal lives off limits to discussion. Go through the following list and check off those topics you would feel comfortable discussing with your best male friend.

_____ my childhood
_____ my religious beliefs
_____ death
_____ problems I'm having at home
_____ politics
_____ my feelings about growing older
_____ my sexual fantasies
_____ money problems
_____ his drinking problem
_____ my fear of rejection
_____ my anger with him
_____ an affair, his or mine
_____ sexual problems, such as impotence
_____ my feelings toward my parents
_____ problems at work

Add up the number of areas you would permit yourself to discuss with your friend. If your total is less than ten, you may be approaching your friendship too conservatively for true intimacy to develop. Do not be afraid to take that chance and open up with another man about your own experiences and problems. You will probably be surprised at how receptive your friend will be to such an overture.

EXERCISE NO. 8

Since I realize that friendships are investments, I am willing to put something down on this one. My initial down payment will be:

_____ I will initiate a heart-to-heart talk.

_____ I will admit my error and apologize to him.

_____ I will tell him how much his friendship means to me.

_____ I will propose fresh ideas for our time together.

_____ I will allow myself to ask him for his support when I need it.

_____ I will show more physical affection.

_____ I will tell him I am angry with him and why.

_____ I will become a better listener with him.

_____ I will stop playing the "Big Brother" role.

EXERCISE NO. 9

Take to heart the American Telephone and Telegraph's message and reach out and touch a buddy from your past. You may have to play detective. Use the telephone information operators, a mutual friend from those days, his parents and family, and the alumni records office of your high school or college. Be persistent. It usually is fairly easy to locate a former buddy. And then call him out of the blue:

"Hi, John, this is a ghost from your past—Carl. How are you doing, fella?"

EXERCISE NO. 10

We all have some special expertise of interest to others. It may be our job (policeman, airline pilot, mammal curator at the city zoo), a hobby (birding, photography, Indian artifacts), or a special skill (white-water rafting, camping, hot-air ballooning). Contact one of your male friends whom you would like to get to know better and share your expertise with him. If you are a fireman, invite him to the firehouse for a tour of the premises and a ride on one of the trucks. Or you may want to invite him to your next hang-gliding meet. Or show him your slides of last summer's backpacking trip to Alaska. Whatever it is, share that special part of yourself with your friend.

MAKING YOUR BROTHER YOUR BEST BUDDY

Brother-to-brother kinship has been the source of some of the great triumphs of history—and its most painful tragedies. A brother is not like a father, although at times he may act like one. Nor is he like a son or a friend, although he may sometimes act like one. A brother is in a special class all his own. Some men would lay down their lives for their brothers. Others hate their brothers with a violent passion, as the homicide statistics verify. Most of us fall somewhere in between these two extremes. Most men will say only that they "get along" with their brothers. "Getting along" usually means there are no ill feelings present. But it also means there are no close bonds. "Getting along" means that we risk little, invest little, and get little from our relationship with our brother.

EXERCISE NO. 11

Where do you stand with your brother, if you have one? The questions below are designed to give you a sense of where you stand with your brother(s).

1. I would describe my relationship with my brother as:

   _____poor _____good _____fair _____great

2. Three things I like about my brother are:
   a) _____
   b) _____
   c) _____

3. Three things I cannot stand about my brother are:
   a) _____
   b) _____
   c) _____

4. When I compare myself to my brother, I always end up feeling
   _____inferior to _____equal to _____superior to him

5. I wanted to be _____ like my brother:
   _____ athletic   _____ tall
   _____ handsome   _____ popular

_____ Mom's favorite   _____ Dad's favorite
_____ a rebel   _____ good in school
_____ smart   _____ happy

6. I still hold it against my brother for _____
   _____ when we were kids

7. The thing my brother and I disagree about the
   most is _____

Look back over your responses. Are there any repetitive themes? How do you feel about the way you line up against your brother? Are you still competing with him, trying to outdo him or feeling outdone by him? If you do, then you are probably still engaged in an age-old sibling rivalry with your brother.

Sibling comparisons, sometimes made inadvertently by our parents when we were at an impressionable age, can come back to haunt us for a lifetime. We internalize our parents' judgments about us as the truth and go through life secretly thinking of ourselves as "the dumb one" or "the wild one." Often these criticisms carry an additional tag: "Johnny, why can't you be more like your brother Paul?" We grew up believing that Paul was doing it right and we were not. Paul won out on Mom's and Dad's approval, while we ended up with a case of sagging self-esteem.

Another thing we should look for in our responses is sibling resentments. Such parental messages from long ago as "Keep an eye out for your little brother" and "Mind your older brother while we are gone" may elicit feelings of affection or resentment later in life. These sibling roles, such as "big brother" and "kid brother," can become restrictive later in our adult lives when we wish to be seen as equals. They become barriers that keep us from really getting to know one another.

THE BENEFITS OF A CLOSE FRIENDSHIP BETWEEN BROTHERS

A reconciliation between brothers can open a brave new world of possibilities. Let's look at a few of them.

- Family ties are often the deepest and most enduring. Our mobile population and lifestyles of today do not afford a sense of rootedness and belonging such as we can experience with our brother. A strong friendship with our brother will put us back in touch with some very positive aspects of our past that we may have overlooked or forgotten.

- Relating to our brother as an adult may reactivate demeaning rivalries, painful comparisons, and dependencies upon parental approval. But the process may present both of us with a unique opportunity to outgrow our childhood fears and insecurities and chuck long-held grudges. Challenged to relate as peers, rather than through their parents, brothers can discover a reality all their own.

- Reconciliation between brothers often has the additional effect of reconciling unfinished business within an entire family. Brothers who rise above petty family jealousies and grudges set a new precedent based on trust, forgiveness, understanding, and love. We free ourselves from the past instead of holding each other hostage to it.

- We gain a trusted friend, a lifelong buddy who also happens to be a blood relative. We are tied to our best friends in a special way because we have "chosen" to be in the relationship with them. While we cannot "choose" our brothers the first time around, we do have the power, as adults, to choose them or lose them.

- Our brothers know us intimately. We share a long and rich history of experiences. We already know about one another the things that it can take years to learn from new friends. We can make this "history" work for us, by building on its positive aspects and updating the old roles and images we have of our brothers.

REACHING OUT TOWARD OUR BROTHER

The first step in ending a grudge or rivalry is to end it in ourself. This means we must be willing to forgive both our brother *and ourself* for the past. It may also mean taking the anger meant for our parents and projected instead on our brother and redirecting it appropriately. We cannot stay angry with our brothers and sisters simply to protect our parents.

EXERCISE NO. 12

It is now time to initiate a contact with your estranged brother. Phone calls are often awkward and too confrontational. Remember—you do not want to be combative. Cassette tapes and letters are excellent ways to initiate contacts of this sort. Begin by making your intentions clear: "I am writing to see if we can forgive one another. I want my brother back." Share your feelings about what has happened and how you feel now. Do not try to cover too much at first. Always end by leaving your brother a full range of options on how he can react to your approach. Do not get discouraged if your attempt first meets with mistrust and suspicion.

The third step is to make plans to get together. There are many more ways two people can connect with one another when they are in each other's visual presence. Try meeting your brother in a place where the two of you shared some good experiences when you were kids. Do not try a reunion of this sort at your parents' home or the home of another family member. The presence of parents or a sister will only complicate matters and interfere with the healing process between the two of you.

And, finally, remember not to expect magic overnight. Take things a step at a time. If you are too anxious yourself, then you will make your brother anxious. The rebuilding of a relationship is a slow process. Be patient!

THE CREDO OF A BEST FRIEND

- I will work and play to make our friendship all that it can be while acknowledging all that it is.

- I will be emotionally honest, even when saying how I feel causes a rift.

- I will cheer my friend's success, recognizing the occasional feelings of jealousy, competitiveness, and fear in myself.

- I will take an active role in defining our friendship by stating what I want and listening to what my friend wants.

- I will accept my friend as he is, recognizing occasional judgments I may make and negative attitudes I may harbor against him.

- I will live by the mutually agreed-upon limits of our friendship, propose changes where I feel they are necessary, and negotiate disagreements in good faith.

- I will accept the ways we are different from one another with an eye toward deepening my understanding and tolerance of things unknown to me.

- I will give unselfishly of myself without expecting a return on my love. What comes back to me is a bonus.

- I will be tolerant and forgiving. Since none of us is perfect, I have no right to expect our friendship will be perfect.

- And finally, I will always remember Ralph Waldo Emerson's words of wisdom: "The only way to have a friend is to be one."

There is a part of our humanity which can only be recaptured if and when we relate with the men of our time. This part of us is nowhere else to be found. Is it not time we resolved to set out in search of that missing piece?

Chapter FIVE

Caution: Men at Work

It was hard to believe what I was hearing. Was it really possible that for two weeks this 45-year-old father of four had gotten up every morning at six-thirty, put on one of his many three-piece suits, kissed his wife and kids goodbye, and then driven aimlessly around the city until the late afternoon when his family expected him to return from work? Could a man actually do such a thing for two entire weeks before he finally broke down and confessed to his wife that he had lost his job? And could this same man, who just months before had been one of the top officers in one of California's largest banks, have fallen into such a deep depression that he would deliberately drive his car off the road at 65 m.p.h.? The answer to all the above questions was, of course, yes.

What is it about our jobs, or the loss of them, that can push a man to the brink, to believe that he no longer has value as a human being and that his life is no longer worth living? What have our jobs come to mean to us as we move through our thirties, forties, and fifties? How can we strike a balance between work and the other important areas of our lives, creating a sense of both internal and external success?

These are some of the challenges confronting men in the eighties, a time when the workplace is undergoing a technological face-lift and a decade when women have carved out a firm place for themselves as wage earners in virtually every profession.

Having come to terms with our feelings, as well as our emotions toward our fathers and other men, we are now ready to take a closer look at the man we are at work. How we feel about ourselves and the progress we are making in our lives is more directly tied to our work than anything else. Work is how we, as men, keep score on ourselves. The work "scorecard" lists job status, salary, title, position, and security under separate categories. As men, we are always checking to see how well or how poorly we are doing in each one, constantly measuring ourselves against our competitors as we strive to "make it" in the world of men.

In this chapter we will tackle these problems and unveil some of the secrets about ourselves that we keep hidden away in the workplace.

LIFESTYLE OR WORKSTYLE: WHICH SHOULD COME FIRST?

Does work fit into our lifestyle? Or does our lifestyle revolve around our job? Do we work to live? Or do we live to work? Is what we call our "lifestyle" in fact only those activities we allow ourself after the demands of our work have been satisfied? When might our lifestyle needs take priority over our job needs?

These are some of the questions that the men of the eighties will continue to ask themselves as the sex roles of men and women change and broaden. The answers, we probably have discovered, are in short supply if we look to our fathers for what they taught us about work and its proper role in our lives.

For many of our fathers, life was work. A man in one of my Alive and Male seminars once told us, "All I can remember of my father was his coming home from work every night. He'd come in the front door about six o'clock each evening. My mother always had a hot meal waiting on the table. After dinner, he'd plop down in his easy chair, read the newspaper, and then fall asleep while watching television. Dad was always gone the next morning by the time we kids had gotten up for school." The same man then admitted, "I could never get away with that crap today. My wife comes home from her job about the same time as I do from mine. And she's as tired as I am. I can't just stand there while she does all the work taking care of the family."

Men today live in a world completely different from the one in which our fathers lived when they were our age. If we relied solely on their rules, we would find ourselves terribly ill equipped to cope with today's challenge of balancing work and home life. Many of our fathers came of age during the Depression or the postwar years. Their chief concern was survival. The working man of an earlier generation fitted himself comfortably in the role of the "male provider," who saw his task chiefly in terms of feeding, clothing, and sheltering his family.

But in today's workplace, with the increasing number of women filling administrative and managerial positions, men face a different set of anxieties than their fathers. The demands of both the job and the family are tearing many men apart emotionally. Do they shortchange their family or their boss? They promise themselves never to be absentee fathers. And yet the demands for specialization at work are greater than ever before. As one man told me, "At work, I think about the wife and kids and worry that I am not giving them enough of my time. But at home, I worry about how far behind I am at work."

There are other anxieties as well, more vague and ill defined perhaps, but real nonetheless. That cold dread when our best friend is suddenly laid off work. The worry that suddenly materializes when we discover that our wife has taken a long lunch with her handsome boss. The churning in our stomach on that morning when our five-year-old cuts herself on some broken glass and the baby is screaming at the top of his lungs just before we take them to the day-care center on our way to work.

As men, we must be able to express these frustrations, uncertainties, and fears. We need, too, to examine our attitudes toward work and the impact they may be having on the other aspects of our lives. And we need to evaluate the extent to which we use the workplace as a secret hiding place. Do our identities at work deny us an even larger part of ourselves?

WORK: A LABOR OF LOVE OR A HIDING PLACE?

Work has become a generic term for what we "do," the place we do it, and who we are. We equate ourselves with our work and take our definition from our job. We say, "I *am* a teacher," "I *am* a carpenter," and "I *am* a minister." For some men work takes on a more individualized meaning than for others. Work may be a "paycheck," a "calling," "a way out," or "a way up."

Is it possible that most of us work because we would not know what else to do? The novelist William Faulkner once observed: "You can't eat for eight hours a day or drink for eight hours a day or make love for eight hours a day. All you can do for eight hours a day is work. Which is the reason why man makes himself and everybody else so miserable and unhappy."

Was Faulker right? Is work simply our chosen way of passing the time of life, filling in the space, keeping ourselves busy, and surviving? What do we have the right to expect from our work in exchange for a lifetime relationship with our job? How much of ourselves should we give up for our work? Before we begin to tackle some of these timely questions, let's answer the question "Why do men work?"

Our work can be either a source of enormous personal fulfillment and liberation or a burial ground for some of our most disturbing fears and secrets. Work should be the stage on which many of our greatest performances in life are given and our most satisfying moments are lived. Men who love their work are often sustained by it through dry spells, losses of loved ones, sudden changes, or crises in other areas of their lives. We have all known someone who "came into his own" largely as a result of his job. Our work can challenge us to use the fullest range of our talents and personalities by helping us to achieve a level of excellence that we would otherwise never have attained.

Ideally, our job does more than provide us with the necessary funds to feed, shelter, and clothe ourselves and our families. True, like our fathers, we must survive. But here are several ways in which work can enrich our lives.

- **We work in order to express who we are.** We work in order to say to the world, "I'm somebody! Here's what *I* do!" Pointing to the fruits of our labor, we exclaim proudly, "This is what I accomplished. *This is me!*" Through our work we distinguish ourselves and become less anonymous. Our work becomes the outer realization of the inner person, a recognizable expression of our existence.

- **We work in order to have a purpose for living.** In the preface to his book *Working*, Studs Terkel describes work as "a search for daily meaning as well as daily bread." We work to make ends meet, both spiritually and economically. Properly done, work can help justify living. Work adds meaning to our otherwise indefinable lives. Human beings need recognition and relevance, order and significance, in their lives. Work can provide all this.

- **We work to feel "a part of" something greater than ourself.** Work connects us to other people. It can be the family at home whom we support through our daily efforts in the workplace or our colleagues at the office. Work binds us to the larger human community. Through work we define a place for ourselves in society. We do our part by putting in "a good day's work." By contributing to the world in which we live, we gain more than money. We also gain a sense of belonging.

- **We work because the act of working is intrinsically satisfying.** Whether we work with our hands, our bodies, or our minds, the process of work is an active expression requiring our talents and abilities. Work allows us to exercise our skills, participate in decision making, and be creative. Activity is synonymous with living.

- **We work to achieve social improvement.** The drive in us to achieve more and better is often tied to our vision of "the good life." To have "the good things in life," we tell ourselves, we must work for them. Social climbing to elevate our status in the community may be as superficial as "keeping up with the Joneses" or as profound as "escaping the ghetto."

- **We work to make our mark on humanity.** Work is our input into the larger world beyond us. Work often enables us to contribute something that will reach far beyond us. As parents give children to the world, workers give of themselves through their work.

THE SECRETS MEN HIDE IN THE WORKPLACE

Unfortunately, too few of us realize these ideals. Our jobs fail to enrich our lives. We look to our work, not as a means to achieve a liberation of some of our better instincts as human beings, but as a hiding place for some of our deepest secrets as men. What are the secrets men hide in their work? Here are several.

Work becomes one more hiding place for our feelings.

Work allows us to avoid many feelings that make us uncomfortable. "Grief, anxiety, feelings of rejection, unfulfilled sexual excitement, guilt, depression, and hostility can be warded off by plunging into work," writes psychiatrist Jay B. Rohrlich, who has his practice on Wall Street, in his book *Work and Love: The Crucial Balance*. The old story about the man humiliated by his boss who comes home and beats his wife is far less common than the opposite: the man frustrated at home who goes to the office and "attacks" his work.

Work becomes a hiding place for our fear of failure.

We bury our fears of failure in our preoccupation with success. We defend ourselves against threatened failure by staying busy. During those times when we think of ourselves as inherently less successful than our colleagues, we overcompensate by working longer and harder. This way our co-workers and bosses will never discover the "terrible" secret we have kept all along—that we feel inadequate to the responsibilities of the position. Salesmen, in particular, have learned that they can bury their fears of failure if they put in the extra hours to exceed their quotas.

We use our work as an excuse not to live more fully in other areas.

Some men throw themselves into their jobs in such a way that it leaves them little time, energy, and interest for either relationships with people outside the workplace or leisurely activities. The appearance of overwork can be the perfect excuse to avoid intimacy. We tell ourselves:: "No time for close relationships now. My job must take priority. But later things will be different." One man I know, an accountant, uses his seventy-hour workweek as a constant excuse not to be up on things. It is his way of saying to the world, "Okay, so I am not an interesting person. But look at my schedule. It's *not* my fault!" And sometimes we flaunt our horrendous work schedule to get off the hook from social and family obligations.

We use work to hide a sense of personal inadequacy as men.

For many men, work is the place where you make your mark as a man. It is the male proving ground which picks up in adulthood where we left off in adolescence on the playing field. Work enables us to become a man. (And, in this view, the home provides a similar sense of importance for women.) For some men, the less secure they are about their status as men, the harder they work. These men's fears and doubts about their worth and status as men are secrets embedded in their drive toward success and compulsive work patterns.

We use work as an indirect expression of love for others.

Many men, especially those in middle age and beyond, have expressed their love indirectly by working long hours and bringing back a paycheck to their families. "Breadwinner's love" is love expressed through a sense of duty and responsibility, often because the man himself does not know how to handle these feelings directly. If asked about this, such a man would probably say that more direct and open expressions of his love—through words and physical contact, for example—are not "his style." Rather he prefers to "show" his love through the sacrifices he makes at work. Hiding his fear and unfamiliarity with intimacy in his job becomes a way of life.

Work becomes a hiding place for feelings of aggressive
competition with fathers, older brothers, former
classmates, and business rivals.

"I'll show that bastard who's the best!" is a common
thought of some men, eager to make a success of themselves at work to prove their worth to others who may
have slighted them at an earlier stage of their lives.
These men find in their work a means of secretly paying
back long-held grudges. This is particularly true of men
with unresolved conflicts with their fathers. Beating out
our fathers for bragging rights in the family, for our
mother's love and approval, or as a statement of revenge
because we feel he did us wrong, places an additional
burden on us at work. For such men ambition is often a
hiding place for a deep-seated competitiveness with their
fathers.

POSTPONING LIFE: ONE MAN'S STORY

For whatever reason you work, all your needs cannot
possibly be met by your job. Studs Terkel in *Working*
quotes a woman who said, "Most of us . . . have jobs
which are too small for our spirit. Jobs are not big
enough for people." And yet there are men who will try
to seek life's riches through their work. These men—and
perhaps there is a little of them in each one of us—will
get so caught up in work that they lose their sense of
balance. Life for them will become, in effect, their
work. They will end up equating the process of living
with the process of working.

Let's hear the story of one man who found himself
trapped in a narrow definition of life as work. Jim Sander-

son today writes a weekly column, "The Liberated Male,"
for the Los Angeles *Times*, which is syndicated to more
than two hundred newspapers and read by over ten million
people. This is his story, as he confessed it to his readers in
one of his most deeply felt and moving columns.

Millions of men are still obsessed with the idea of
"making it" or "being somebody." You always start with
the idea that you'll work harder (and be smarter) than the
next guy. You work long hours and never sleep much. Your
mind is always churning up new ideas, battle plans, and
competitive fears. It's a relief to leap out of bed and get
moving each morning. You don't have to like your work.
You just have to be good at it. Moving up in the world is
all that counts.

Some mornings I'd get to work so early I'd pass the
hookers coming in from a long night in midtown. At times
I'd think that maybe deep down we were a lot alike—they
sold themselves for money at night; I sold myself during
the day.

But there were good times as well—the euphoria of
pitching a new account and winning, of pushing our gross
up another notch, of making our little company noticed in
the industry. Sometimes the good feelings would last for a
couple of days . . . or a couple of martinis.

But in the end there was always that nagging feeling
that I still wasn't moving fast enough. Every setback so
savagely depressed me that the only answer was to work
harder. I spent such long hours in the office that I never
saw my kids awake. I would sneak into their bedrooms at
night with a tiny flashlight to look at their sleeping faces
and reassure myself that they were still alive.

Some dim voice of conscience pleaded with me to get
out of this kind of life. But I always rationalized, "I've

come this far. I can't go back now."

When you hear the words "push, push, push" pounding inside you like a giant heartbeat, when you don't have the time any longer to play with your kids, to spend an evening making love, to rejoice or commiserate with a friend, then you certainly do not have any generous emotion to spend on a stranger. Art? Music? Reading for pleasure? "What's the bottom line on all that? Where's the payoff in the real world?" I'd ask myself.

Needless to say, I was not a very good husband during that time of my life.

"What is it that you really want?" my wife once cried in desperation one night.

"A million bucks," I told her.

"Then what will you do?" she wanted to know.

"I'll start living," I replied with no hesitation at all.

Some men have to have a heart attack before they suddenly realize they must change or they will lose everything. For me it was the shocked look on my wife's face. She didn't say anything as she stood across from me. There are moments, horrifying epiphanies, when no words are needed.

In the end it was not as hard to get out of the business and find a new career as I had thought. I've spent several years now rediscovering the real world. I've done a lot of searching back, too, to try to learn when and why I decided material success was worth paying any cost to achieve.

Life is so short and precarious that we are fools if we do not constantly examine the meaning of our harried days. Few people are ever satisfied with their success, no matter how grand. You never really "make it" because your goals keep reaching ahead of you. And if in trying you lose love and your humanity, then you've lost it all.

EXERCISE NO. 1

Let's take time out for several exercises that will allow you to assess where you stand in regard to your work. Here are some questions that will help you clarify your approach to your work. Be honest, now, in answering them.

First, let's determine which side of the fence you are on in the "love of work" area. On the one side we have the TGIF (Thank God, It's Friday) Man, who lives for his weekends and has little emotional attachment to his job. On the other side is the TGIM (Thank God, It's Monday) Man, who lives for his job and finds it painfully difficult to downshift when he is off work. Smack in the middle is the man who has achieved a balance between the two extremes. He enjoys his work during the week but also values his leisure time. Position yourself on the graph below, making a mark where you honestly think you fall.

TGIF	TGIM

*　　*　　*　　*　　*　　*　　*　　*　　*

EXERCISE NO. 2

On a scale from one to ten, one being "completely uncertain" and ten being "completely certain," how sure are you that you are in the right job now?

1　2　3　4　5　6　7　8　9　10

(uncertain)　　　　　　　　(certain)

EXERCISE NO. 3

1. You have come to the end of a busy day on the job. You worked hard and were productive. But much remains to be done.
   a) Do you tell yourself to "do more" and stay on the job several additional hours?
   b) Or do you pat yourself on the back for a good day's work and then head home to spend the evening with your family or friends?

2. You are working against a deadline and the pressure is on. You struggle to create the right solution to a particularly sticky business problem.
   a) Do you muster all your resources and power through to a solution?
   b) Or do you step outside for a few moments for a breath of fresh air and the chance to clear your mind temporarily of all work-related problems?

3. Your closest friend at work is given a promotion and a substantial increase in salary.
   a) Are you jealous because you did not get the raise you had expected?
   b) Or are you happy for him?

4. Your company hires a younger man to do essentially the same work you do. You see him making a disastrous mistake which might destroy his credibility in the organization.
   a) Do you let him fail so that you in turn will look better?

    b) Or do you help him out and avert this potential disaster?

5. You have had a bad day at the office. Your boss unfairly blamed you for something that went wrong. It eats at you the rest of the day.
   a) Do you take your pent-up frustration home with you and dump it on your family?
   b) Or do you stop off at a city park on the way home and walk your frustration off?

6. You are at your twentieth high school reunion. You discover that a good friend from those days who had been voted the "man most likely to succeed" has been nickel-and-diming it as an actor and part-time schoolteacher.
   a) Do you inwardly look down on him, feel sorry for his failure to establish himself as a success along traditional lines, and perhaps flaunt the signs of your own material success (an expensive German car, a good salary, a big home)?
   b) Or do you try to get to know him better and gain some understanding of why he has chosen to go into acting and teaching?

7. You have not taken a vacation with your wife in over five years. Your business is going well. You have a good cash flow coming in. You know you can afford a good vacation now. But you wonder if you can afford the time away from work.
   a) Do you postpone the vacation indefinitely in your mind and buy your wife a piece of jewelry with the extra cash?

b) Or do you set aside a week on your calendar, slip the airline tickets into a dozen roses, and hand them to your wife?

8. Do you get unduly irritated when you get caught in a traffic crawl on the way home from work, when you have to wait at a checkout counter, or when you have to wait to be seated in a restaurant?

_____ yes   _____ no

9. Do you like to do two things at once, such as read while you eat, shave in the car on the way to work, fill in a crossword puzzle while listening to music, or think about business while playing golf?

_____ yes   _____ no

10. Do you have nervous tics? For example, do you often catch yourself slamming your hand on the table to make a point, grinding your teeth, clenching your jaw, or making a fist?

_____ yes   _____ no

11. Do you find that you see less and less in your environment? After you have visited an office, store, or home, do you discover later that you cannot describe the decor and furnishings of the place?

_____ yes   _____ no

12. Do you feel vaguely guilty when you relax and think that there are other ways you could utilize the time more productively?

_____ yes   _____ no

If you have more than four answers in the "a)" and "yes" categories, then perhaps you should reevaluate what is setting the tone for the way you live your life. Like many men, you may be letting your workstyle dictate your lifestyle.

WHERE DO WE GO FROM HERE?

The respective seasons of a man's life are largely shaped by his job and society's expectations for a man his age. A man in his youth is assumed to be busy carving out his place in the world of work, while the older man is expected to relinquish his. A man's job not only sets the pace and tone of his life, dictating where he lives and the kind of husband and father he will be, but often determines the longevity of his life. Many men's jobs are of such a nature that when they are asked to relocate, change shifts, or alter their basic lifestyle, they have little choice but to comply.

For many of us men life is (or has become) work. We define ourselves and our lives on the basis of what we do for a living. And this inevitably costs us some of our humanity. When a man becomes heavily dependent upon his work for his sense of personal worth, he often equates the loss of his job with the loss of his place in the world. He ends up in Nowhereland without a sense of purpose for living, whirling in confusion and feeling displaced.

How might we approach our jobs so that we can have success without becoming dangerously dependent upon our work? What other themes besides work can we thread through our lives to become more well rounded? How can we break free of the restrictive stereotypes of what a man in our age bracket "should" be doing at a particular stage and time when they do not fit what we personally want for ourselves and our families? These are some of the major questions we will want to take up.

"I AM NOT MY JOB; YOU ARE NOT YOUR JOB!"

What is the most common piece of information you discover upon meeting another man for the first time? Not his name, age, or marital status. No, it is his occupation. His job. When we meet another man for the first time at a social gathering, our first question is almost always "What do you do?" The answer—teacher, carpenter, doctor, taxi driver—gives us an immediate handle on the other man, allowing us to place him into a category and assign him a label. And that label provides us with clues that tell us how to act, what to say, and what to expect of the man we have just met.

Labels can be terribly destructive things. Like all stereotypes, they have the effect of making the other person "invisible." We lose sight of his individuality and see only what our prejudices predetermine us to see.

"Labels affect how you perceive the other person, which in turn influences what you hear," insists Dr. Kermit Moore, a professor in interpersonal communication at the City University of New York. "Regardless of the label, it prejudices—which literally means to *pre*-judge—you toward the person. Thus, you tend to focus on information that confirms the label."

I am convinced that knowing another man's occupation is the *least* effective way to get to know him. It sets up a comparative and often a competitive basis for the new relationship. I say this because most men are prejudiced against other men when it comes to the question of jobs. We typecast one another, as if we are privy to universal truths, such as "All bankers are tightwads" or "All car salesmen are shysters" or "All doctors are snobs." These hidden occupational stereotypes and the readiness with which we position other men in the great hierarchy of professions keep men from relating to one another as people.

In my Alive and Male seminar, I ask participants at the beginning *not* to reveal their occupations when they introduce themselves to the group. Almost at once the men feel awkward, as they grope toward alternate forms of identifying themselves. Some are at a complete loss. The men quickly begin to understand how much they automatically define themselves—and, by extension, others—by their occupations, how much we stereotype other men and close off from them if we do not feel they are "suitable."

Without the job titles and the arbitrary status they confirm, the men in my seminars enjoy a fresh new experience with their fellow males. Free from the restraints imposed by the knowledge of other men's professions, they learn they can get at the real story—the dreams, the joys, the fears, the frustrations, and the achievements that nobody had ever noticed before. As one man put it, "I was surprised to learn that the inner life of a carpenter is no different from that of a surgeon." And it is this inner life that gives men not ordinarily accustomed to opening up in the presence of other men the common ground to share the most intimate details of their past and present lives. Then, and only then, can these men start to relate, *really* relate, to one another. (Of course, this ability to relate sympathetically and with apparent ease is often associated with the most respected and successful businessmen.)

Then at the end of the day I ask each man to announce his age and occupation. Aside from an occasional "I could never have guessed..." and an "I just knew he had to be...," the room is still. After the last man has finished, I ask for a moment of silence in which each one of us can reflect about the changes in us and the group.

At a workshop in Colorado, one of the participants told the group he was a judge. That stunned everybody. Some of the men were immediately intimidated and threw up an emotional barrier between themselves and this man. Others resented him. The judge became quite angry and pleaded with the group, "I do the work of a judge. But I am a person. The most important thing about the experience today until now has been to have you people as my friends. For God's sake, do not turn me out now simply because I told you what my job is."

In another Alive and Male seminar in Philadelphia, two long-time business competitors found themselves together for the day. Curiously enough, while they had built up a fierce competitiveness and dislike for one another over the years, they had never before met face to face. During the day they struck up a friendship, neither one knowing what the occupation of the other was. At the end when we announced our last names and jobs, these two reacted with shock and disbelief. And then they had a good laugh on themselves. "For ten years I hated this guy without ever knowing him," one of them told the group. "And suddenly today I find I like him. Who would ever have thought it possible?"

At another seminar two participants who chose each other as lunch partners discovered later in the day they had an equally unusual situation. The older man in his late sixties and the younger man in his early thirties looked like the "odd couple" of the group. But they quickly developed an affectionate, playful, and joking rapport with one another. When the group divulged their occupations, the young, ambitious lawyer and the semiretired Superior Court judge soon discovered that they had a date in court the next week. "Out there in the real world where occupations count, we probably could never have started this friendship and discovered how many interests we shared," the judge insisted at the end of the day.

Our occupations can do much to bring us closer to other men. But we must constantly remind ourselves that a man is much more than his job and strive to learn about that part of him which is not covered by his job. And we should never allow our preconceptions and prejudices about certain kinds of jobs to prejudge the suitability of another man for friendship.

Let's try several exercises to help us break through this job barrier that men put up between themselves and other men.

EXERCISE NO. 4

Because this exercise requires a small measure of deception on your part, you may feel uncomfortable. If so, then pass over it to the next exercise. However, people who have done this exercise have found it to be a useful and powerful learning experience.

The next time you find yourself on unfamiliar turf, perhaps at a party where most of the people are strangers, assume a different occupation with the people you meet. When men or women ask you what you do, tell them you are a taxi driver, a lawyer, or a travel photographer. Make mental notes of how their reactions to you differ depending upon whether the profession you have picked is glamorous and prestigious (a doctor, a Hollywood assistant producer) or not.

EXERCISE NO. 5

Women learn to draw men out, asking questions about their work which help these men feel important. In doing so, they break through to the person behind the job. He opens up because someone has taken an interest in him, via his work. We can learn from women in this area by asking more pointed and more personal questions the next time we are introduced to another man. Avoid the temptation to get stuck in small talk about jobs, sports, or the weather. Begin by asking personal questions about his work. Some possible questions to begin with: "Do you like your job?" "What other job would you rather work at if you had the freedom to change?" "What are you the most proud of at work?"

A variation on this is to ignore completely the question of profession when introduced to another man. Do not tell him your profession or ask his. Rebuff all questions from him on the subject. Instead, resolve to learn as much as possible about him as a person, his interests and activities away from the job. Do not be shy about asking personal questions. The results may surprise you.

EXERCISE NO. 6

Set up a lunch date with a male colleague at work, preferably someone you have known and worked with for some time. Be casual: "Say, Paul, how about keeping me company for lunch today?" Before you go, make a list of all the things you know about your colleague *as a person*. This should include whatever facts of his private life, early life, and interests outside of work you already know. For example, is he married? If so, does he have children? How many? What's their sex and age? And so forth. If you are like many men, you will find yourself with a sparse list. At lunch, avoid all work-related topics and seek out the man behind the job. Ask him about his special interests or hobbies. Draw him out. And if he starts to wax enthusiastic about, say, photography, let him talk and ask additional leading questions. Then after lunch, make a second list of all those new things you learned about your colleague *as a person*. Compare the two lists and note the differences.

EXERCISE NO. 7

Another highly effective way you can humanize the workplace is by inviting someone special—your wife, children, or a close friend—to visit you where you work. Let them see firsthand where you work and what you do. Some companies encourage this. The San Diego Gas and Electric Company, for example, has a successful program in which its employees can bring their children to spend the day with them on the job, whether they are linemen, repairmen, secretaries, or managers.

Jack, a lineman, brought his eight-year-old son, Randy, to work with him one day. It was a moving experience for both of them. "At first I thought it would be no big deal," Jack admitted later. "My kid sometimes asked questions about what I did. So one day I said, 'Hey, you want to know? Come and spend the day with me.' In we went at seven-thirty one morning. He made the rounds with me and my partner in the SDGE truck doing repair work. Randy's a bright kid and asked a lot of questions. He took a real interest in my work. And the funny thing is that I had been getting bored with the job. But seeing it through Randy's eyes gave me a new way of looking at my own work. Now when I go home Randy often asks me questions about my day's work. I can talk about some of those things with him and he understands. In fact, that day on the job with my son went so well that three weeks later my partner brought his ten-year-old daughter to work with him.''

BECOME INTERNALLY SUCCESSFUL NOW

Internal success is knowing that we are successful *now*. Not when we make a million dollars. Not when we are elected to the City Council. Not when we have been made a partner in our law firm. And not because we have put in thirty years with our company.

Success should be a state of mind first before it blossoms into an external manifestation. The only way to be truly successful is to think and feel successful. Our sense of success should reside within us rather than outside in our titles, power, status, or the things we buy with our money.

Most of us have been taught to work to *become* successful. The idea of starting work each day *as* a success requires a completely new orientation in our thinking. We resist the idea of thinking of ourselves as successful now. Success is usually something that comes to us at a future date, something we are still working toward.

Let's take a few moments out and entertain the possibility that success is a *process* rather than an *end point*.

The first step toward a redefinition of success to make it work for us is deciding exactly what it is we want in life and from our jobs. "Success," as the world judges it, is fruitless and empty unless it is also seen as success by the individual. Of what value would a Rolls-Royce and a home in Beverly Hills have been to the nineteenth-century philosopher Henry David Thoreau, who once wrote, "A man is rich in proportion to the number of things he can afford to let alone"? On the other hand, would John D. Rockefeller have counted himself a success because he had the love and respect of humble men and women?

Here, as elsewhere, we cannot lose sight of the fact that we are in charge of our lives and the values for which we live. We must decide the specific criteria for our success, not let others decide for us. Only then will we feel truly successful. Men who achieve great wealth, power, or fame and still feel empty have sought after someone else's idea of success, not their own. When they get it, they fail to be fulfilled. "Is this all there is to my success?" they ask themselves in despair and frustration.

How can we avoid that state of quiet desperation that comes of knowing too late that we have exhausted our time, energy, and resources seeking after that which, once obtained, fails to give us the deep satisfaction we longed for? A first step here is to take an accounting of what exactly we want from life—not what the world, our wife, parents, or friends expect from us.

EXERCISE NO. 8

Here are some things to take into consideration in regard to your work. Put a check beside those items that you rate most important to your personal sense of success and an X next to those items that mean little or nothing to you.

Forget what other people want for you or what you have been told you should want. Still that clatter inside your head for a moment. Listen carefully to what that voice inside you says. Do not edit what that voice tells you into a compromised version. Listen to the voice. And accept the truth of what it tells you.

What I really want the most in life is:

_____ love

_____ fame

_____ parental approval

_____ recognition

_____ to make it to the top

_____ to impress people

_____ to serve God

_____ to be happy

_____ to feel productive

_____ to experience pleasure

_____ to be a good husband

_____ to achieve excellence

_____ lots of women

_____ many friends

_____ other: _____

_____ _____

_____ money

_____ power

_____ respect

_____ to help others

_____ a big house

_____ an expensive car

_____ to be my own boss

_____ to make others happy

_____ to be creative
_____ to be proud of my work
_____ to be a good father
_____ to travel widely
_____ a good education
_____ good health

_____ _____
_____ _____

Go over the list of things that you checked off as the most important to your sense of success. Don't be afraid of your responses if you do not fully understand why you selected them. Trust your unedited instincts. Look at the list carefully. Examine it. Let yourself feel your choices. Imagine how your life would be if you actually obtained all those things that you checked as the most important to your sense of success. Now might be the time to rewrite your scorecard.

Remember, the point of life is to enjoy it. All other goals, be they money, fame, status, or achievement, are merely ways of making you happy and are worthless in themselves.

Once you know what it is that you want from life, then you can figure out how to go about it. Remember that success is an ongoing process. Milestones are fixed points of reference. Take things one step at a time. We all want to see if there is going to be a big payoff out there in the real world. Will it arrive in the form of a weekly paycheck, a standing ovation, a completed project, a promotion, or a repaired pipe? How will the world know that you have been successful? Some results are more tangible and immediate than others. But always remember that you alone must decide whether you are a success or not. As one man told me, "I work because I feel successful. My success is not up for grabs. I determine my success."

EXERCISE NO. 9

Now let's do several quick exercises to determine if your job will allow you the opportunity to achieve the kind of success you want from life.

Of those things I rated as the most important to my sense of personal success, my job will help me obtain the following:

1. _____

2. _____

3. _____

4. _____

5. _____

Of those things I rated as most important to my sense of success, my job will either block me from obtaining or at best do nothing to put me closer to achieving the following goals:

1. _____

2. _____

3. _____

4. _____

5. _____

EXERCISE NO. 10

The three things I like the most about my job are:

1. _____

2. _____

3. _____

The three things I hate the most about my job are:

1. _____

2. _____

3. _____

Look over the data generated by the last three exercises. When you tally up the pluses and minuses, will your job, as you have now defined it, contribute substantially toward your goals of success? You may have an ideal job. If not, can you see ways in which you can change your situation within your present line of work to make your job more satisfying to you?

If you think that the odds are against any real changes taking place that will make your present job satisfactory, then perhaps you should give some hard thought to changing jobs or maybe even careers. This obviously is never an easy solution. It requires considerable risk, courage, and a strong belief in yourself to succeed. This is also an excellent topic to take up with your wife, buddy, or father. The reward of a major job overhaul or a minor job adjustment can be a revitalization of your life.

THE HUSBAND WHO WALKED AWAY

Let's look at the story of one man who completely reshuffled his life. Several years ago, Scott, 46, without warning to his seventeen employees, abruptly sold the prosperous retail business he had spent most of his life building up. That night, less than a week before his twenty-fifth wedding anniversary, he announced to his wife what he had done and told her that he was moving out of the house to live as a single man. The next day he notified his two children in college that they would have to take out loans on their own to finish their education. The money machine had gone out of business.

Stories like this are usually presented as "male menopause" horror tales. But let's hear Scott's side of the story. I offer it here as an extreme example of what happens to those men who keep a secret too long and do not seek sooner a midpoint correction of their lives.

"Some men sell their businesses. And some men leave their wives. However, I don't think many do it in one day. In my case, the reason our marriage lasted as long as it did was because I was always working so hard. I knew I could never make it once I had retired and was home twenty-four hours a day. So I told my wife we should live apart until we both had made some changes in our lives. We may not even get divorced. At the moment she is not pushing it.

"Of course, my wife suspected another woman was involved. But that was never the case. I certainly wanted more sex and did seek out new partners after I had settled down on my own. But in the end, there was no desire left in our marriage anymore. It got to the point where I had to sell my wife on the idea every time we made love, which was about once a month. A lot of men my age discover that they have been starved of powerful sex for years, and they decide to do something about it. Now I've met some women who haven't given up on sex. They're playful, inventive, and even aggressive sometimes.

"But I did not make all those changes just to get more sex. I don't know what did it finally. Some straw broke the camel's back. I do know that one morning I jumped out of bed before dawn and threw on my clothes, my mind panicking with all the things I had to get done that day. When I got downstairs, I discovered it was only 3 A.M.

"In all, I had twenty people riding on my back, emotionally and financially. We were just like a family in the store. We celebrated birthdays and weddings, and they'd come to me for advice, even though some are older than I am. They couldn't believe it when I said I couldn't take those fourteen-hour days anymore. Inflation was killing us. We had to get bigger in a hurry, which meant a huge bank loan at those sickening rates, and another mountain of worry for me to shoulder.

"Or we had to cut back. And that would have

meant firing people, some of whom had been with me for over fifteen years. They didn't listen to me. They never heard what I was saying to them. It didn't matter to them that I sold out cheap to a big chain operation with a good pension plan and a strong union to protect them. All they knew was that Big Daddy had bugged out. He wasn't going to be there anymore to take care of them.

"And my wife and kids felt just as betrayed. Everybody was absolutely outraged at my selfishness. It didn't matter that I was on a treadmill running like a squirrel and every year the mill turned faster. I think they really stopped seeing me as a person. I was just a part of the machine that provided all the options in their lives.

"The funny thing is that for years I never minded. In fact, I absolutely loved it for a long time. Much later I came to feel that we were all playing out a script that someone else had written for us. I think the script called for me to have a heart attack when I was about 52.

"When I look back over my life, there were three or four points when my wife might have convinced me to ease up, to take a different path with less pressure. But she never really tried. I used to come home and tell her about what was going on in my life at the store. But after a few years I could tell she really was not listening. She couldn't even keep the names of my key people straight. She was absorbed into her own world of the kids, her gardening, her music, and playing tennis at the country club.

"We don't have enough to retire on. I suppose that sooner or later I'll have to get another job, but I don't

know when that'll be. My blood pressure has fallen
way off, and I am in better health now than I have
been for years. For the first time in my adult life I'm
trying to make each day a precious experience, instead of deferring all my pleasure to some vague date
in the future. It's finally my turn to have some options in life, too."

Scott's story illustrates what happens when men allow a
bad situation at the office to continue indefinitely. Had he
made some changes earlier, then he might well have saved
both his marriage and his career. The time to handle such a
crisis is now. Men must not permit the situation to deterio-
rate, as Scott did, to the point where only the most extreme
options remain.

STEPPING OFF THE TREADMILL

Men who drive themselves to exhaustion always have a
thousand and one excuses as to why they must keep running on their treadmills. "I can't let up now, not after all
these years." Or: "It'll just be another few years. Then
everything will be all right, and I'll start to live." Or:
"What would I do with myself? My work has been my
whole life." For these men, and Scott was one of them, it
usually takes a crisis with their health or marriage to convince them that their work priorities are not the only ones
which need attention. And even then they step off the
treadmill reluctantly.

Mark, a salesman for a computer company in Los Angeles, is one who made that decision to ease off earlier
than most. "Last year I turned 35, and it scared me a little

bit. I decided to make it my push year—you know, working sixty to seventy hours a week. It was like running in a marathon. Well, I found out that I could do it. I raked in over $75,000 in commissions and got a bonus. Later the company offered me a regional sales rep position. You know what? I turned them down. I could have done it. But I decided that it wasn't what I wanted. I just didn't want the big office, secretaries, and the extra bucks. I realized that I wanted to enjoy life more than I had been, to read the paper and play with my kids. I missed my two boys. Now I have more time to build my relationship with them. Sometimes I feel guilty, like I should be out there hustling up business for sixty hours each week like I used to do. My best friend even thinks I blew it. But I discovered that it was not what I really wanted."

Let's decide that we do not want to wait to be hit by a crisis before we change. Here are several suggestions that may prove useful.

We can change our non-work activities.

Let's schedule in time for a walk through the park, a bike ride in the country, reading a novel, an evening class in painting, or anything that requires slow and easy participation. We can lean down hard on ourself to follow through on these "time-outs" from our regular routine after work or on weekends.

We must get away from the telephone.

Workaholics are most often slaves to the telephone because it allows them to maintain contact with their office from home or elsewhere. Cordless telephones and computers may serve the same function. If we are sincere about learning how to relax, then we are going to have to cut the cord, so to speak. We can use a telephone answering device or service to field our calls. When we go on vacation, we can stay at a lodge or hotel without telephones in its rooms. And we can let the telephone ring without picking it up. Remember—other people can and will learn to deal with matters after we are gone from this earth. We are dispensable. And even if we are not, most business can wait. We will never learn this until we experience it. So, painful as it may be at first—let's get lost!

We can make special agreements with ourself for rewards.

Let's allow ourself special time off for extra effort put in at work. We can set up our own reward system for the good work we do by paying ourself off with something very personal and enriching. Let's treat ourself to that weekend fishing trip, day off in the middle of the week, time spent with an old buddy, or dream vacation with our lady friend that we have been promising ourself. The trick here is always to pay up. There are so many times when we put in the work and postpone the rewards. Let's not cheat ourself. Let's keep that contract we made with number one. We deserve it!

We can keep anti-anxiety focus cards handy.

One method many men have found extremely effective in making changes is to prepare a set of three-by-five "focus cards." These cards serve as reminders about the positive attitudes and behaviors that they are actively working to incorporate into their workstyle. Well-placed focus cards with simple messages can do a world of good. Some suggested messages are: "Relax," "I can't be everything to everybody," "I have accomplished enough for today," "Work *can* wait," "People will still love me if I'm not perfect," and "Breathe easier." If used faithfully, these cards will help us replace such counterproductive, anxiety-provoking messages as: "I am not doing enough," "Make more, better, and faster," "Hurry up; you're behind," and "Push harder, harder, and harder."

We can learn to enjoy leisure time.

Too many of us think of "leisure" as the negative of work and not as its true opposite, something positively defined in itself. Let's widen our cultural and intellectual horizons—the areas where there is no immediate tangible payoff, no bottom line. We can learn to balance times of activity with times of rest through passive action. Passive action means that we become actively receptive, receiving rather than giving out energy. Being passive is difficult for many men because they perceive it as time wasted. But learning to take something back from the world after putting out so much all day restores the necessary balance we need to work effectively. Well-spent passive time off the job can make us more productive and creative on the job.

Here are some examples of things to do:

1. We can treat ourself to a delicious, healthful gourmet dinner. Let's pick a restaurant with mood music in the background, soft light, and a leisurely pace. We will do everything at one-half or one-quarter speed. Let's chew our food slowly, savor each bite, and rest between each course. Spend at least two hours eating the dinner.

2. We can go for a one-hour deep-muscle massage. Then we will close our eyes and simply yield ourself up to the massage. We will let all the tension flow out of our body. We will rest, relax, and enjoy ourself.

3. For a change of pace, let's set aside thirty minutes in which we do absolutely nothing. We will stop all activity and just be. We may find ourself squirming uncomfortably the first few minutes. But we will stick with it. We will keep our mind from focusing on business. We will clear our mind of all thoughts. Or if that is not possible, we will just focus our imagination on a peaceful scene, such as an alpine meadow full of wildflowers.

4. We can go for a long walk. In this time we will allow the world to make an impression on our senses without trying to make something of the experience. Many people do this while jogging, biking, or sailing.

BEING OUR OWN MAN AT WORK

Being our own man at work means doing what gives us pride and pleasure as well as profit. It means that we have our individuality, as well as our mutuality, as a member of the work team. We are attuned to our own thoughts and feelings about what is happening at work and express them effectively through the appropriate channels. We may or may not be our own boss, but we are unmistakably our own man at work. In other words, we are taken seriously by others. We, in turn, take other people seriously. We arrive for work with a positive mental attitude, focusing on present tasks without interruptions from past fears and future anxieties. We balance our desire for excellence with a high regard and appreciation for the process, or means, by which it is achieved.

After doing all we can to assure the best product or service, we acknowledge ourself and others who have contributed and then call it a day. We leave work feeling exerted yet invigorated. Our excitement at what is to come in our time away from the workplace makes itself felt as we leave the office. The evening, or weekend, we have planned is evenly balanced between passive action (rest and replenishment) and play and activities. If we are returning home to relationships, we do so feeling ready for making contact, prepared to represent our needs, and open to the needs of others.

Chapter SIX

Sons and Lovers: The Mothers in Men's Lives

MOTHERHOOD, APPLE PIE, AND A SUICIDE NOTE

Recently, I reread a suicide note written by David, who early one Thanksgiving Day took his life by leaping off the Golden Gate Bridge while on a trip to San Francisco. His tragic decline from one of the city's finest citizens and businessmen to a life spent in and out of psychiatric hospitals had become more than he could bear. David's suicide note, written just hours before he jumped, reflected the thoughts of a painfully tormented human being. But in those final moments, David's mind had become clear.

Because I had been David's friend and therapist, his parents shared his suicide note with me several weeks after his funeral. It took several readings before I realized that he had written the note to his mother. It did not begin, "Dear Mom." Nor did it say anywhere, "This note's for you, Mom." But there was no question that the person who figured most prominently in David's thoughts those last few hours was his mother. Despite his staunch independence and seeming detachment from his mother throughout his adult life, David's final gesture was an acknowledgment of his mother. She was his first, his last, and in the end his most enduring connection to life.

The cord that unites mother and son may be Western society's most powerful bond. In her excellent book, *Mothers and Sons*, Carole Klein gives several striking examples. General Dwight David Eisenhower took time out from the planning of the Allied invasion of France in May 1944 to send a Mother's Day greeting to Ida Eisenhower in Kansas. Industrialist Andrew Carnegie's mother begged him not to marry until after her death; he waited one year after she died and finally wed for the first time at the age of 52. In the early stages of his political career, Franklin Delano Roosevelt made few important decisions until he first talked them over with his mother; when he and Eleanor fell in love, Roosevelt was so concerned about his mother finding out that he wrote about Eleanor in code in his journal. And actor James Dean once apologized for his troubled life by saying, "My mother died on me when I was nine years old. What does she expect me to do? Do it all alone?"

Most of us were born to mothers whose primary job in life was to take care of us and keep house. Mom was ever-present, accommodating our basic needs as children and providing us with the practical skills we needed to take those first steps out into the world. Her direct involvement in the everyday matters of our lives kept us in constant, close personal contact with her. Whether the memories of our mothers are good or poor, she had a profound impact upon all of us.

Our purpose in this book has been to turn our secrets into powerful new truths for men to live by. Throughout we have focused on ways in which men can better themselves psychologically while at the same time they improve their relationships with their fathers, male friends, and work. As men's needs in these areas become healthier, their relationships with women benefit. They come to them with more to offer and greater receptivity to what is offered in return.

Men's secrets with and about their mothers need not accompany them to their graves, as in the tragic case of my client David. His hidden desire to reconnect with his mother, as well as his growing helplessness, were secrets that he could not bring himself to share while he was still alive.

This chapter focuses on men's secrets toward their mothers. We will strive to clean up the clutter in our relationship with that woman who gave us life, our mother. We have known for a long time about the importance of the mother-son bond. But what is its impact upon men's subsequent relationships with women? What can men do to keep their relationship with Mother separate from those with other women?

Earlier we examined how many men experienced their fathers as physically or psychologically "absent." This left them yearning for a model of what it meant to be a man. Because many fathers were effectively "absent," their sons often entered into unspoken and secret agreements with their mothers to fulfill those needs left unsatisfied. But try as hard as she could, Mom could not fill in for Dad in all areas, for she lacked that prerequisite quality of maleness that Father possessed. Often our anger with Mother for what she could not give us (that is, our father) is really misplaced anger at Father for "stranding" us. Mother ends up taking the rap for Father. And in the process we sometimes lose sight of her own unique contributions.

Let us begin our personal investigation by reminding ourselves that, regardless of what happened between us and our mothers, our happiness today is our responsibility. We must understand the nature of our mother-son relationship without casting blame on Mom for what she did not know, could not help, or was not able to control. And we need, too, to understand the extent to which our picture of Mother is a product of our perception of her rather than the reality.

MAN TO MAN

First let's hear what several men have had to say about their own mothers. Once again, other men's experiences, whether similar to or different from ours, can often remind us of the universality of some of our own deepest feelings.

> "My mother was an angel. I don't know how she did it but my mother put up with us four kids and stayed married to my dad for thirty-five years. It wasn't much of a life for her. But you never heard her complain."
>
> George, 36, a machinist in Seattle

> "I left home when I was 16 years old. Today my mother and I live two thousand miles apart. I call her only once a year, on Mother's Day. Even then, I'm very tense. I don't know why. I only know that I had to put two thousand miles between us before I could feel comfortable."
>
> Jack, 32, a stockbroker in Denver

"Mom raised four kids on a teacher's salary after my father's death. She worked harder than anyone I know for us kids. I'll never be able to express enough appreciation to my mother for what she did. I respect that woman an awful lot."

Carl, 41, a school administrator in Atlanta

"At times, my sister would get so angry at me I thought she wanted to kill me. She got the short end of the stick in my family. I got all the attention. Her achievements never seemed to mean as much as mine. I felt bad for her because my sister had to do twice as much to get half the attention from my mom. I think it was because I was her son."

Charles, 29,

a maintenance supervisor in St. Louis

"My mother had both an excellent education and an extraordinary talent as a pianist. But she got married shortly after college and spent the next twenty years of her life raising us two kids. She was bored so much of the time. I was her favorite kid. My mother always wanted me to be a big success. She told me that if I did well she would feel redeemed. I know now that I went into medicine more for her than me."

Peter, 38, a surgeon in Boston

"I was my mother's only child. She was a sickly woman much of her life. And yet she rarely complained. I had this dream as a kid of living in Europe for several years to study art at one of the academies there. God, how I wanted to go. But I could never bring myself to travel too far away from Mother. I knew that she would think I had abandoned her. And so I stayed close to home. She had done so much for me I really felt I owed her that. My mother died when I was 32. By then, I was settled down in a good job with my own wife and kids. It was too late for me to get to Europe in the way I had hoped as a kid."

John, 38, a magazine art director in New York

BORN INTO THE MALE MYSTIQUE

My friend Bonnie recently told me of a disturbing incident that occurred between her and a friend. Both women have two daughters and share everything from mother-daughter outings to car pooling. Bonnie's friend became pregnant again and gave birth to a son this past year. After hearing her friend state emphatically for the third straight time, "Bonnie, you just don't know how wonderful it is to have a son. You're not really fulfilled until you've had a boy," Bonnie became angry. "She's either intimidated by having a son or there's a mystique to baby boys," Bonnie told me.

Bonnie said the incident reminded her of the times she had visited her grandmother's house when she was a kid. "When I would visit, my grandmother put fish sticks in the oven for dinner, but when my brother arrived, she'd roll out the red carpet," she remembered. "As a child, I was jealous. But today the more I think about it, the more I would not have wanted that kind of pressure on me."

Recent surveys show that some 80 percent of Americans want their first child to be a son. And while we might expect this attitude among traditional males, the same studies also show that only one woman in ten prefers to have a daughter first. There is no doubt that having a male child has a unique social and psychological meaning for many women. For some, a son means a sense of completeness. "A son is the clay with which many women fashion their most intricate life designs," Carole Klein states in *Mothers and Sons*. One of her subjects confessed to her: "It is as if, through him, I've found the missing half of myself." The feeling of creating a lost half sometimes accounts for the extraordinarily close relationship between some mothers and sons, as these mothers sought to make their mark through their sons on the male-dominated world about them.

Born into the male mystique, many men are commissioned from an early age to go out on a secret mission for Mother. This mission may be something as simple as succeeding in a profession Mother would have pursued had she been a man. Or it may be as complex as trying to shape themselves into the kind of man Mother *really* wanted to marry. Often men do not know what drives them to please and impress women, or to rebel against them. In reality, it is because they often are unknowingly carrying out Mother's "secret assignment."

Our mothers had a vital influence on how we perceive ourselves as men and the male roles we went on to assume as adults in our own families. In order to square with ourselves, we must come to terms with our mothers—not only our mothers as people but the mother in us. Similar to the "father in us," our relationship with our mothers affected the way we are with ourselves.

What did our mothers teach us about growing up male and about what it was like to be female? Were they proud and happy to be women or sad and unhappy? How did our mothers feel about our fathers and men in general? Did we feel that our mothers loved us? How did they express their love? Through food? Touch? Conditionally on the basis of how well we "performed"? Did they teach us how to love ourselves as males or to apologize for being male? Did our mothers expect us to be like, different from, or better than our fathers? Or did our mothers want us to be simply ourselves? Did we get all the mothering we needed? Or did we feel shortchanged? (And, as a consequence, do we look for mothering in our adult relationships with other women?) These are some of the questions we will want to examine in order to come to terms with our mothers and the women in our lives.

HOLDING MOTHER HOSTAGE TO OUR EXPECTATIONS

"If, as a boy, a man had a relationship with his mother that was nurturing but at the same time allowed him some opportunity to test his own strengths and abilities—if she struck the right balance between caring for and letting go —then he'll relate to other women in a healthy way," observes New York psychologist Eric Margenau. "He'll choose a girlfriend or wife on her own merits—neither substitute for, nor rejection of, his mother. The relationship won't turn into an unconscious game of either putting the woman down for things that his mother did or trying to turn her into his mother. He won't have to relate to a woman on the basis of a lingering image of his mother at all. On the other hand, if the dynamic of a man's interaction with his mother was unhealthy in some way, then the points of unresolved conflict are going to enter his life with the next woman, and the next, and the next."

Men do not often discuss their unresolved feelings about

their mothers. While they play a key part in their relationships with other women, these emotions are often hidden away out of our awareness. Men's deepest feelings toward their mothers remain some of their best-kept secrets, even from themselves. Yet a large part of what men expect from women, and of themselves as men, dates back to their childhood experiences with their mothers.

For example, we may have seen our mother as a woman who defined her role along traditional lines. Such a mother may well have gone about her business of cooking, cleaning, chauffeuring, and orchestrating her children's daily lives with a sense of acceptance of her lot in life. Motherhood was her calling in life, and she took great joy and satisfaction in seeing it done well. Her husband always found his "castle" in good order when he returned from his workplace. Occasionally, this mother would "raise her voice." But more often than not, she remained good-natured and even-tempered. Such a mom was careful not to "burden" her children with her problems. This "Good Mom" lived for her family, even when that meant sacrificing her own needs. She took the accomplishments of her husband and children and made them her own. When they were happy and doing well, then she knew that she had done her job. She was supportive and accepting, and her children were always sure of her love.

The son of such a mother generally has a sense of himself as an individual, separate and apart from his mother, yet related to her in healthy ways. He has a solid, basic trust in women. He likes women, enjoys their company, and is ready to make a commitment. He has good skills of communication which come in part from having had a model of disclosure who has given and received clear messages.

But what if we perceived our mother in a somewhat

different light? Suppose we saw her instead as a woman who sacrificed her needs for her family but was determined to make her husband and children pay for it by playing out the role of the martyr? She may have constantly reminded us of all that she had done for us, seeking to induce guilt, elicit sympathy, and reinforce feelings of indebtedness. Or she may have suffered deliberately and silently, developing chronic ailments or depression. Whichever it was, "suffering" became her way of controlling others and drawing attention to her needs. Never would she take responsibility for her own unhappiness. Rather, she always made her husband and children feel they were at fault.

A man who perceives his mother along these lines may well end up with feelings of guilt and a sense of lifelong indebtedness that make him think that nothing he can do, give, or say will be enough to satisfy his mother. Such a man will often exhibit a sense of guardedness, anger, and resentment toward women in general along with a fear of committing himself to them and thus risk "losing" his identity.

Or suppose we saw our mother as a woman who was overly protective, a woman who took her natural protective role to an extreme? She was convinced that something "bad" would happen to her son unless she was there to protect him. She was on a twenty-four-hour guard watch, taking even the most minor threats as confirmation that the world is, indeed, a dangerous place. This kind of overly protective mother often did not allow her son to go out for sports because "he might get hurt." Even when her son becomes a man, she continues to watch over him as though he were still a child, projecting her feelings of helplessness, powerlessness, and fear on to him.

My Uncle Irv, a dentist, once told me the story of one of

his patients, a 74-year-old man whose 93-year-old mother lived in the building next to his dental office. One day the man came in for his regular checkup. After he had driven off, his mother quickly hurried over to my uncle's office. "Tell me, Dr. Schuster," she inquired, "is my son taking good care of his teeth?"

Such a mother often will not let go of her son, keeping him tied to her apron strings. Her message is: "Don't grow up!" Men with such mothers frequently lack self-confidence. They have a sense that they cannot make it on their own and need their mothers there to take care of them at crucial times. They still unconsciously accommodate their mothers' directives to remain helpless and dependent, but now they do it in their adult relationships with women. The price these men pay for this care is high. Having grown dependent upon others to take care of many of their needs, they put themselves in a position of powerlessness.

How can we begin to free up what we feel, good and bad, about our mothers and enjoy improved relationships with both them and the women in our lives? Here are several exercises which will allow us to start to get a handle on our feelings toward our mothers.

EXERCISE NO. 1

List below or in your journal the three most important characteristics of your mother which best define her as a person. For example, you may recall her as a loving and intelligent woman who, nonetheless, "babied" her husband by catering to his every whim.

1. _____

2. _____

3. _____

EXERCISE NO. 2

List below or in your journal three experiences you had as a boy with your mother that provoked feelings of love, warmth, and security. For example, you may remember fondly those times when you were sick and confined to bed (with extra pillows and some toys) and your mother fussed over you continuously, bringing in special meals on a small tray and giving you her undivided attention.

1. _____

2. _____

3. _____

EXERCISE NO. 3

List here or in your journal three things you think a mother should do for her son that your own mother might have neglected with you. For example, perhaps your mother worked all day instead of staying home with her kids, when that was what you, as a boy, wanted. Or maybe you regret that your mother never stood up for you with your father. Whatever the lapses, recall them now.

1. _____

2. _____

3. _____

EXERCISE NO. 4

My experience in counseling men has taught me that the majority of problems men have with women stem from the relationships they had with their mothers. Many of us are still tied secretly to our mothers in a variety of ways that we may not want to admit to ourselves. We set up expectations with our wives and women friends that are based on our relationship with our mothers.

How can we tell whether we are still tied to our mothers in ways that prevent us from having intimacy with other women? Here is a checklist that may prove helpful.

I am still tied to my mother in the following ways:

_____ financially

_____ to approve my choice of a spouse

_____ to approve my lifestyle

_____ to approve my choice of friends

_____ to approve where I live

_____ to approve my appearance

_____ to approve my religious practices

_____ to approve my style of parenting

_____ as my primary source of love

_____ for my self-esteem

_____ by my fear of abandonment

_____ by competitive feelings with her

_____ by my anger and resentment

_____ by my need to rescue and protect her

_____ for my basic care

_____ as a go-between between myself and my father

_____ by her power over me

_____ by my fear of her dying

_____ by my guilt

_____ because my father neglects her

_____ because she is lonely

_____ from fear of her disapproval of my values (sex, drugs, lifestyle, etc.)

SECRET WARS WITH MOTHER

We know about the "real" wars some men carry on with their mothers. Angry words are fired in salvos or dropped like bombs. Amid the carnage of the battlefield mothers disown sons, and sons disown mothers.

Others of us wage secret wars on our mothers. These are silent wars, acted out only in our minds. In these secret wars we are the writer, producer, director, choreographer, and actor. We get to play both protagonist and antagonist, editing in imaginary lines for cruel mothers to speak, so that their victim-sons might rise up against them. Daily, we battle Mother's presence in our minds, fighting off the criticism we still hear ringing in our ears, her overprotectiveness that taught us to mistrust our instincts, and the burden of guilt she tried to lay upon our shoulders.

"Love-hate relationships" are often born out of silent wars. Men who secretly are at war with their mothers feel love on the one hand and hatred on the other. One side yearns for Mother, fantasizing an ideal mother-son relationship. The other side is repulsed by her, seeking vengeance on the woman he blames for everything that went awry in his life. The battle rages on secretly inside him.

Men who become fantasy soldiers in an imaginary war against their own mothers are unwilling to risk the little security they feel they have. But they need some way to do battle with what they perceive as their mothers' destructive behavior toward them. Secret wars are their chosen defense against the women who would threaten them.

The key factor in ending these wars is to bring the battle aboveground. We must first become conscious of what we are doing and then how these feelings manifest themselves in our present relationships with women. Once we have understood the two warring sides in us, we are then in a better position to negotiate a just peace. We must never forget that it is acceptable for us to have feelings of both anger and love toward our mother. Each side has its own point of view that deserves to be heard. But each side must be made accountable to the reality of our mother as a person.

CLEANING HOUSE WITH MOTHER

A first step toward reconciliation with our mother is to acknowledge and then let go of our grudges toward her. This is not an easy thing to do. But resentments often prove a heavy burden to carry through the years. And they stand in the way of our positive feelings toward our mother. By acknowledging and then letting go of our grudges, we can often simplify our relationships enormously.

Below I have listed some of the most common grudges men have expressed toward their mothers. Check the ones that apply to you.

1. _____ "I resented the way she came between me and my father."

2. _____ "She treated my father like dirt. No woman is ever going to treat me that way."

3. _____ "My mother always let my father push her around. I hated being around when that happened."

4. _____ "I can never forgive my mother for letting my father treat me the way he did. I've never gotten over it."

5. _____ "My mother never really grew up. I always felt like I had to be her 'Little Man' and take care of her."

6. _____ "My mother always took terrible care of herself."

7. _____ "She worked too hard all her life and never took anything for herself. Even when I became an adult and had a good job, she refused to let me do anything really nice for her."

8. _____ "My mother could have been a great dancer. But she gave that all up to get married and have kids. She wasted all that potential."

9. _____ "My mother was much too protective of me. At times I felt like she was going to suffocate me. She never let me do anything for myself."

10. _____ Other: _____

_____

_____

As with Father, we are faced with a choice. We either hold Mother hostage to our resentments. Or we understand and accept her reality. A resentment-free slate with Mother may lighten the burden for other relationships cluttered with unfinished "mother business." Or if we cannot completely rid ourselves of all our resentments toward our mother, at least we can try to balance them off against the good she did. That way they become more manageable.

EXERCISE NO. 5

Make a list in your journal of all your grudges toward your mother, much as you did with those you held toward your father. Now write down exactly what your mother must do for you to forgive her. Try to be as objective as possible. Are your expectations realistic, based on what you know about your mother? If your expectations are reasonable, then discuss them with your mother, making clear to her, politely but firmly, exactly what she can do to heal the breach. On the other hand, requests to your mother made from the point of view of an eight-year-old child will not be met. If your conditions for a reconciliation are not realistic, then revise them to conform to the point of view of an adult.

PAYING OFF LIFELONG DEBTS TO MOTHER

Some men have so armored themselves with anger or indifference toward their mothers that they claim not to feel anything for them. Other men spend an uneasy lifetime feeling indebted to their mothers and later to women in general. This indebtedness often exists only in our minds, as we seek to reconcile ourselves to all that Mother "sacrificed for us." Some of us may have had a mother who actually preyed upon our guilt.

Let's rid ourselves of that burden of debt we may feel toward our mother. By expressing our gratitude—if not directly to our mother, who may be dead, then to another woman who can symbolically accept it on her behalf—we may experience one way of settling our "debt." Thanking our mother, as one adult to another, is one way of breaking unhealthy ties and might provide the opening needed to allow us to start establishing healthy ones.

Remember—it is much easier for the human computer to retrieve resentment than gratitude. But resentments serve absolutely no helpful function in the long run.

EXERCISE NO. 6

Let's use this opportunity to take a full inventory of the gratitude you may feel toward your mother. The following checklist should help.

I am grateful to my mother for:

_____ her encouragement
_____ her patience
_____ her warmth
_____ her cooking
_____ her love
_____ her strength
_____ her dedication
_____ her hard work

_____ her good humor
_____ her leadership
_____ her courage
_____ her wisdom
_____ her honesty
_____ her attentiveness
_____ her support
_____ her good housekeeping
_____ my life
_____ her care when I was sick
_____ her protection
_____ her spiritual influence in my life
_____ my education
_____ my brother(s) and sister(s)
_____ marrying my dad
_____ teaching me about girls
_____ her generosity
_____ helping me with homework
_____ reading me stories
_____ exposing me to _____
_____ buying me a _____
_____ showing me how to _____
_____ being such a good example of _____

Once we understand the many forces affecting our relationship with Mother, we are now positioned for the next step—accepting the past. We may not agree with it. And we may forever wish it had been better. But it happened. And unless we wish to have it also be our future, we must at some point accept it.

We must express our acceptance of our relationship with our mother as best we can. Perhaps she will not understand or accept an expression of reconciliation. In either case we must clear our minds and hearts of the mother clutter that inhibits our expression of love and compassion toward women.

Here are several exercises that may prove useful. Remember—our purpose should always be reconciliation, not confrontation.

Write your mother a letter

Sometimes the best way to begin clearing the air with your mother is to write down all your thoughts in a letter. Without pulling punches, say it like it is. Almost immediately, you should feel some relief. Half the time when I have written letters like this, I never send them. I feel so much better at having expressed my feelings that actually mailing the letter is anticlimactic. But when I do want a response or a dialogue with another person, this is frequently the most effective way to go about it. When I have recommended letter writing in the past, some people ask, "But why not have it out face to face?" The answer is clear. A mother who receives a written correspondence has time to go over it several times. When the same thoughts are expressed in person or over the phone, she may not understand them as well as she would upon reading and rereading your letter. Letters are an excellent medium for mother-son housecleaning.

Write up focus cards

Again, focus cards may serve an important purpose as we begin to steer ourselves away from the "old," approval-seeking behavior and strive to replace it with "new," self-supporting messages. One man I know kept an "I approve of myself" card in his hand during long-distance telephone calls to his mother, whose disapproval was the unconscious object of his fear for thirty-five years. Keep these cards near the phone during the times you talk with your mother.

Have a mother-to-son talk

Comparable to the "man-to-man" talk recommended earlier for men and their fathers, a direct, face-to-face meeting with Mother may prove the most confrontational and yet most rewarding of all the approaches. To ensure the best results, you and your mother need to agree in advance on both the objective of the talk and the ground rules. This may seem excessive. But let me assure you that the most successful "peace talks" are those in which all the players play by the same rules and have a keen sense of their objectives. Here is a checklist that you may want to cover to get the best return on your investment.

a) Decide the issues and list them. Stick to the issue at hand until both of you decide to go on to the next item on the agenda.

b) Decide beforehand how long the talk will last. Come up for air by taking periodic rest breaks.

c) Determine the ideal time and place for the discussion. Restaurants, with other people in close proximity and the high level of background noise and other distractions, are not the best places.

d) Avoid "control tactics" such as interrupting, accusing, dominating, withdrawing, or attacking one another.

e) Keep in mind at all times that the chief purpose of the meeting is to bring this discussion—hopefully, the first of many—to a positive conclusion. Your intention must *not* be to turn the talk into a courtroom or battlefield where it is decided who is "right" and "wrong." Rather, you wish to make peace with your mother.

Take your mother to lunch

Sometimes the simplest of gestures, like taking her to lunch, a movie, or an event she loves will do more to bring a mother and son closer than a direct confrontation over the issues separating you. Tell your mother that you have put aside a half day just for her. Then ask her what would be a special way for the two of you to spend that time.

THE BENEFITS OF A RECONCILIATION WITH MOTHER

- **I gain another facet of my relationship with my mother.** As a friend, I add a "bonus" dimension to a lifelong association with my mother. We become honest friends, willing to take risks, enjoy a great time together, discover new things in common, reminisce, and explore one another's lives more fully. As two fully formed human beings, Mother and I grace one another's lives with a unique brand of love and affection, acceptance and respect. We build upon the old bond a new one that is relevant to our lives as they are today.

- **More sharply defined boundaries with my mother add definition to other close relationships.** I also get to enjoy a rewarding adult relationship with my mother independent of, and yet in no way competitive with, my father and my wife. Because I am not ambivalent about my "place" with my mother, my other close relationships benefit.

- **I gain a loving mentor who knows me intimately.** I get to benefit from my mother's years of experience and accumulated wisdom, as well as her personal interest in my welfare. Mother is more attuned to who I am, having known me longer, better, and in more ways during my maturing years than anyone else.

- **I gain a trusted confidante.** My mother and I are freer to take each other into our confidence, call upon one another for favors, and rely upon each other without feeling trapped, taken for granted, or overextended.

And finally, let us remember the words of writer Anne Roiphe: "All of us, men and women, carry our childhoods with us forever. Memories shape our character and affect our present actions and feelings. But as we reach maturity, we have to take responsibility for our own lives. It may be hard to look at our rough side, but inevitably we all must confront the past and say how much it will direct the future."

Chapter SEVEN

Men's Life Partners

"Women are just too much trouble"—anonymous male

"Men are just one big pain"—anonymous female

"Relationships are just one big hassle"—anonymous couple

These are difficult times for relationships between men and women. Each generation works out its own "game rules" (called sex roles) to cope with some of our basic differences as men and women. We are taught to play by the "rules." But in a relatively short time the "game" has been redefined and the "rules" changed. Relationships bear the brunt of these changes. Amidst our uncertainty of how to "play" at our relationships with the other sex today, we often find that such qualities as patience, tolerance, and flexibility are in short supply. Marriages that we thought were "perfect matches" suddenly come apart at the seams. The divorce rate in some states matches the marriage rate. To meet the challenge of our changing times and values, we need to achieve a higher level of communication and to demonstrate a willingness to keep the dialogue alive.

In this chapter we will focus on ways that men can achieve greater intimacy and satisfaction in their relationships with their "life partners." A life partner is someone with whom we share a committed, ongoing relationship. She may be a wife or a girlfriend. Men face two major problems in dealing with life partners. They allow their unresolved feelings toward their mothers to clutter up their relationships with other women. And they often have real difficulty approaching their wives and girlfriends free of destructive images, fantasies, and expectations that allow little room for a woman's true self to emerge.

SIX SECRETS THAT MEN HAVE IN REGARD TO WOMEN

1. **Men may say that they want "Womanlove," but what they really seek from women is "Motherlove."** "Motherlove" is like no other love a man will receive, and he knows it. This unique quality of love comes but once in a man's life. Never again, as adults, do men receive the attention and care they got as children.

   Men who did not get the mothering they needed, or who became addicted to that which they did get, secretly pursue this "Motherlove" in their adult relationships with women. These men pass up "Womanlove" in a search for the all-

elusive "Motherlove." They feel they have a right
to caretaking from women. Or, as one of my male
clients succinctly put it, "women *owe* it to men to
take care of them." The traditional elements in
society reinforce these men's view that "a
woman's place is in the home, taking care of her
family's needs." These men commission women
(including their daughters) to administer them a
regular fix of "Motherlove" each day. (These are
the same men who often get upset when their dinner is not ready on time.)

2. **Men simultaneously want and fear being taken
   care of by women.** There is a hidden desire in
   most men to be loved and fussed over by a
   woman. There is nothing like the tender, loving
   care he feels resting in her arms or the feeling he
   has when he walks through the door after a hard
   day's work and smells fresh blueberry muffins.
   ("Just the way Mother used to make them!") On
   the one hand, men want to turn themselves over
   to somebody else's care. To do so, however, also
   means handing power and responsibility for their
   basic needs over to another person. This is when
   many men panic and begin to feel trapped.

3. **Men hide their desire for romance.** The politics
   of being a man call for men to play down their
   natural romanticism and sensuality. "Only sissies
   become sentimental," men tell themselves. "Soft"
   is a four-letter word to be excluded from a man's
   vocabulary. Many men stifle their romantic feelings and let them peek forth only on special occasions. And even then it may be difficult for them
   to say, "I love you," except indirectly by sending

flowers, candy, or a greeting card (written by somebody else).

4. **Men grow secretly resentful of the roles they play with women.** Men and women are taught from early childhood what their "job" is. Men who grew up believing that their job is to provide for their families have a deeply ingrained sense of responsibility to do just that, week after week, month after month, year after year. Women who grew up believing that it is their "job" to attend to their family's every need also feel a duty to serve in that role day after day. Women's "job resentment" is today an open secret. But what about the men? Many of them, too, feel resentful, disenchanted, and trapped in their "jobs" as the family provider.

5. **Sometimes men do not want sex.** There are times when men simply are not in the mood for sex. They may be tired, angry, emotionally upset, or merely disinterested. Or they may prefer to be tender without having it lead to intercourse. There are also times when men use sex to reduce tension, not to "make love." Because many men are afraid to say "no," they push themselves to perform in bed when they do not want to. Men who cannot say "no" to their partners become prime candidates for sexual "burnout" (erectile dysfunction and other forms of impotence). Such a man may not be able to say "no," but his limp penis (just like an erect penis!) has a mind of its own. When men allow sexual prowess and performance to become a central measure of their masculinity, they often defeat their own cause by pressuring

themselves into wanting, or appearing to want, sex on all possible occasions. Sooner or later in every man's life, his body speaks out in defiant rebellion, his flaccid penis emphatically stating, "NO!"

6. **Men sometimes fake orgasms.** If you believe that women are the only ones faking orgasms, think again. The truth is that some men have difficulty achieving an ejaculation and are afraid of losing face with the woman. Or, they end up faking an orgasm to give their partner a sense of having done her job well. Men who feign orgasms do so because they have decided they are better off faking one than having to deal with a wounded ego.

Let us now look more closely at the biggest secret in men's relationships with women, their hidden emotional dependency upon their wives and lovers, and its chief cause, the unresolved business toward their mothers.

THE MAN IN THE GRAY FLANNEL PAMPERS

"Jack can be so infuriating at times," a highly successful career woman in San Diego once told me in exasperation. "On the one hand, he is strongly supportive of my career in banking. And yet he still assumes that the shopping, cooking, and cleaning are my responsibilities. Maybe I shouldn't be surprised. I learned long ago that there is a little boy inside every man I've ever known. Even the big, strong, tough men need you to do the smallest things for them. I can always see it coming—Mommy Time."

Men for years have tried to project an image of themselves as strong and independent. But women have never been fooled. They know that even the most powerful men are dependent. A woman friend calls this the "Gray Flannel Pampers Syndrome." The mistake of most women has been to assume that the men themselves realize how dependent they are. But few do.

Too many relationships end up today with the woman shouting, "You don't want a woman; you want a mother!" This sense of learned helplessness in such critical areas as self-care, parenting, and housekeeping forces many men into an unhealthy dependency upon women. If a woman confronts a man on this score, the chances are that he will shrug off any criticism with a comment such as "Blame it on my mother; she spoiled me." Time and time again, women find themselves forced to jostle with his mother and other women in a competition to take care of their man's needs.

What are some of the ways in which men are dependent upon women to fulfill their emotional and physical needs? Since we men like to present a picture of ourselves as strong and coolly independent, even to those closest to us, it is sometimes hard to tell. Hard, that is, unless you live with us. Men disguise their dependencies well. We may depend upon women for the "little things." For some men, this means a warm meal every evening and stacks of clean shirts in their bureau drawers. For others, it may be the softness we allow ourselves to feel when we are next to her softness. The story of what happened to a neighbor of mine illustrates this well.

After twenty-five years of marriage, Al and Jan decided to get a divorce. Their children all grown, they discovered they had little else in common. They sat down with their lawyers, drew up the papers, and divided their property. They had shared many turbulent years together, but the pre-divorce arrangements went smoothly. Al and Jan found separate apartments. Everything went well until an incident occurred that forced Al to confront his dependency on Jan.

Al's new car had been in the repair shop for several days. He had a doctor's appointment in the heart of San Diego, a good twenty-five dollars away by taxi. He called Jan and asked her to drive him to the doctor's office, wait for him, and then take him home again. Jan, who had always been available to help Al with the "little things," refused to help him out then, saying she had other plans. Al was upset. His wife had always adjusted her schedule to meet the demands of her family. But Jan was acting on the advice of her friends and making an effort to break her ties with Al. After all, they were divorcing and she had to learn to live her own life.

Al was outraged. "What do you mean, you've got other plans?" he shouted at her. "If you think I'm going to pay fifty bucks for a cab, you're out of your mind."

Al felt helpless and hurt (and fifty dollars poorer) afterwards. For the first time in twenty-five years, Jan was not there when he needed her. The incident threw him into a terrible depression.

Underneath his outrage and disappointment was a scared little boy, much like the little boy he had been as a child. Al's mother, overwhelmed by the demands he made upon her as a small child, responded to him in a way that left him feeling rejected, with the sense that he was too much trouble. Since then, Al had decided not to make demands on people, even though this meant denying some of his own needs. He was always afraid of being a "bother."

To "need" was not just dangerous in Al's mind. It was a sign of unmanliness.

With Jan, Al had established a lifelong relationship in which it had become safe for him to let a woman take care of him. In all other areas, he had remained staunchly independent, refusing to let other people do even the smallest thing for him. He had come to see Jan's caretaking as an expression of her love. Even though they were going through a divorce, Al felt betrayed and unloved when she refused to take him to the doctor's office. He felt cut off and was forced for the first time to face how emotionally dependent upon her he had become.

Fortunately, Al was able to confront his hurt and dependency needs. Today he looks back on the incident as an important learning experience. "It was a lot easier hurting than it was fooling myself and everybody else all the time," he admitted to me. "Having admitted it, at least now I'm in a position to do something about my pain."

Perhaps if Al had been more aware of his feelings of dependency, he would have been less devastated when Jan finally chose to act independently. We need to come to terms with our dependency. Once we do that, we will be free to become "interdependent" with our partners, meeting each other's needs out of mutual acceptance and understanding.

PUTTING MOM'S FACE ON OTHER WOMEN

There is another danger men and women face when men expect their life partners to pick up where their mothers left off. Sometimes men secretly punish their wives and women friends for their mother's "crimes." They may find themselves becoming unusually pushy, defensive, angry, overly sensitive, and frustrated with little or no provocation. Something their wives or women friends do or say suddenly lights a short fuse inside them. The anger, frustration, and confusion that may result is but the ghost of those feelings they had years before in encounters with their mothers. These youthful emotions will continue to haunt them and the women in their lives until they learn to recognize them for what they are and face their feelings toward their mothers.

How do these ghosts manifest themselves? Writer Anne Roiphe offers up a poignant story about one such encounter with a ghost-ridden male: "A man I once loved was a terrible miser. He counted out the tip for the waiter in pennies. He shopped at ten supermarkets to save on each of their specials, and stored junk mail to use as stationery. While financially comfortable himself, he had experienced poverty as a child. He remembers his mother collecting pieces of string. He remembers her talking animatedly about the wonderful bargain she found here or there. His economies turned out to be both a way of pleasing his mother and a way of preserving her within him. As he slowly counted out the bits of silver in his pocket, he felt close to her again."

Mother's ghost can take a thousand and one forms. The man who turns his wife into a permission giver has yet to exorcise his mother's ghost from his marriage. Men with controlling mothers may secretly promise themselves never again to give that much power to any woman.

Whether our experience with our mothers has been good or bad, a precedent has been established. The stage has been set for our subsequent relationships with women.

These closely guarded secrets about our mothers prevent us from realizing the full potential of our relationships with other women. We hide them by putting up walls.

THE WALL OF MOTHER

The Wall of Mother is maintained by the man with split loyalties. He is in love with two women and, if that is not enough, one of them happens to be his mother. Because he is still tied emotionally to his mother, he cannot fully commit himself to the other "special" woman in his life. Good old Mom is his ace in the hole. If things go wrong in his relationship, he can always go home to Mother.

The man who erects the Wall of Mother does not usually recognize it until his wife, once enthusiastic about making his favorite food, suddenly announces she is "sick and tired" of competing with his mother's meatballs, matzo balls, wontons, or pecan pies. He may not see the competitiveness until he is struck by his mother's cutting tone of voice as she points out his wife's shortcomings. This man finds himself in a difficult, if not impossible, predicament. He is asked to choose between his mother and his wife, both of whom he loves dearly.

THE WALL OF HELPLESS DEPENDENCY

The Wall of Helpless Dependency is another favorite with men who have failed to reconcile themselves with their mothers. These men ask to be taken care of by women rather than assuming primary responsibility for their basic needs. They eventually become burdens to themselves and to their women. We hear their sad lament in the lyrics of the popular songs that pour forth from our radios. The male vocalists cry out in song after song, "I'm lost without you, baby. Can't you see I'm hooked on your love." The secret we have hidden all along, that men rely upon women more than we care to admit, comes out in these sad songs.

The extent of our dependency comes home only when we suddenly lose that special woman in our life. Then our world collapses around us. At that point we find we must fend for ourselves. Sometimes even the simplest house-keeping chores become insurmountable problems.

On the day before he was shot to death, former Beatle John Lennon confessed to an interviewer the shock of his discovery of his dependency on his wife, Yoko Ono: "The worst [part about being separated] from Yoko was realizing that I needed her more than she needed me, and I'd always thought the boot was on the other foot. Yoko kicked me out. I said, 'Okay, okay, I'm going. I'm a bachelor, free.' I've been married all my life, so I'd never been a bachelor since I was twenty. It was god-awful."

THE WALL OF GODDESS WORSHIP

This scenario works itself out something like this: A man meets a woman, falls in love, and shapes her into something superhuman. She becomes a goddess in his fantasy, an ideal vision of the perfect woman. She can do no wrong. Such a man leaves his real flesh-and-blood woman no chance to be her normal, imperfect self. His impossible standards do not allow it. Eventually, reality breaks through. His goddess proves human after all. But the goddess worshipper cannot tolerate any imperfections. He feels betrayed, even though the woman may have done nothing more than act human. The romance ends abruptly.

Why do these men engage in a persistent, futile search for the perfect goddess? Once again we come back to Mother. "Our first concept of our mothers is someone all-caring, wise, omnipotent," insists Anthony Pietropinto in his book *Beyond the Male Myth*. "Some men try to recapture this fantasy of the mother who always knew what to do."

Needless to say, the Wall of Goddess Worship is yet one more way that some men block true closeness and intimacy with their life partner.

THE WALL OF ANGER

When a man has suffered wounds in his relationship with his mother, psychological scar tissue is left. To prevent further injury, such a man will often erect the Wall of Anger. His mother may live three thousand miles away or she may have been dead for twenty years. But the wall stands as a monument to past mother wars. Tragically, the wall also shields him from his wife or women friends. Men like this are usually unaware of how angry they actually are and how their anger serves to keep women at arm's length.

CHECKING FOR MOTHER IN OUR RELATIONSHIPS WITH OTHER WOMEN

Are we secretly putting our mother's face on other women?

Below is a checklist of feelings to look for in our own behavior with our mother and other women. No single one alone is evidence. But several, taken together, may reflect a pattern of unfinished business with Mother that is disrupting our relationships with other women:

_____ I seem to be angry with women in general. I feel hostility toward my wife or girlfriend for no apparent reason, but usually find some excuse to justify my angry feelings.

_____ My relationships with women tend to turn into power struggles. I am constantly striving to assert my authority.

_____ I find it difficult to trust my wife or woman friend, even during the best of times. No matter how hard women strive, they can never do enough to win my confidence.

_____ I feel alone even when I am with my wife or woman friend. I also know that she can never really understand what I am going through. But then, I have never tested my theory by opening up to her with an honest expression of my feelings.

_____ I still try to outdo my brothers and sisters to get my mother's attention, cutting them down whenever the opportunity presents itself.

_____ When people ask me about my past, I always tell them the "tragic" story how my mother victimized me. I repeatedly portray myself as the "perfectly innocent" child victim.

_____ I find myself making cutting remarks about my mother or someone else's mother.

_____ I avoid contact with my mother whenever possible.

If men clean house with their mothers now, they will open the doors to more positive feelings about women in general. Finishing "mother business" is like clearing a cluttered desk. Unresolved emotions, like work that piles up, only serve to remind us how far we are behind day after day, year after year. Clearing the slate of useless anger, bitterness, resentment, and fantasies about our mother can make all the difference in our relationships with other women.

THE ROAD OF DEPENDENCY VS. THE ROAD OF INDEPENDENCE

"I swear, my first husband believed in house fairies— the Dirty Shirt Fairy, the Dust Fairy, the Button Fairy, the Vacuum Fairy, dozens of little fairies who magically appeared from nowhere to get all the housework done," my friend Carmen, a manager with a high-tech company in San Jose, California, once complained to me. "My husband was an engineer, and yet he was absolutely helpless when it came to matters of daily living in our home. After ten years of marriage, he still had not learned how to operate our washer and dryer to do a special load when he needed it. He had no domestic survival skills, whatsoever. When we divorced, he had a very tough time for a while. He simply could not take care of himself. Of course, he finally found another woman who would."

Are we men really helpless when it comes to meeting our basic needs? Are we incompetent at taking care of our children? Have we been rendered unfit by our genes and hormones to wash and wipe up?

We cannot expect to progress further in our relationships until we overcome our crippling dependency on women to take care of us. Many of us do not admit it, but we are secretly intimidated by everything from Cuisinarts to the latest-model coffee makers. Learning the basic skills necessary to take care of ourselves does not mean being "cut off" from some of the special things we have enjoyed receiving from women. It simply means that we have begun to confront our learned helplessness. By involving and empowering ourselves, our dependencies and fears are broken one by one. We start to feel competent preparing food, caring for children, performing basic household management, and relating to others socially.

EXERCISE NO. 1

The place to start is by taking an honest inventory. What are the areas in which we are dependent?

The basic care I'm unprepared to provide for myself is:

_____ washing my clothes

_____ ironing my clothes

_____ doing simple repairs on my clothes (sewing on buttons, repairing tears, etc.)

_____ preparing delicious, nutritious meals

_____ shopping intelligently for food

_____ washing dishes (by hand)

_____ operating the dishwasher

_____ keeping a clean house

_____ vacuuming the rugs

_____ keeping the kitchen tidy

_____ cleaning a toilet bowl and shower/bathtub

_____ balancing the checkbook

_____ organizing an interesting vacation

_____ keeping my financial affairs in good order

_____ living within the limits of my income

_____ handling wisely my investments

The ways I am unprepared to provide basic care to others are:

_____ changing diapers

_____ feeding an infant

_____ bathing a child

_____ reading to a child

_____ playing with a child

_____ tending a sick wife

_____ planning a family vacation

_____ caring for a sick child

_____ cleaning up after a sick child

_____ making coffee for guests

_____ giving a good massage

_____ preparing a family meal

_____ doing the family laundry

_____ providing first aid to my kids

_____ doing simple household repairs

_____ organizing a large party and preparing the food

_____ supervising my kids for several hours or days at a time

_____ helping my children with their homework
_____ keeping the financial affairs of my family in
            good order

EXERCISE NO. 2

Having taken an inventory of those areas of self-care in
which you depend on others, you may wish to start a program for developing some domestic survival skills that will
allow you greater autonomy in the conduct of your own
affairs.

The three areas of domestic self-care in which I would
most like to develop greater competence are:

1. _____

2. _____

3. _____

Now let's set about developing that competence. If you
are a single man, then perhaps until now your idea of dinner has been a hastily prepared sandwich, washed down
with a beer, or a box of fried chicken, salad, and rolls from
the nearest fast-food outlet. You may envy your male
friends who can whip up a delicious repast with little effort
and would like to do the same. If you are married, then
perhaps you depend upon your wife for all your meals.

Regardless, you may wish to set aside one evening in
the week when you learn to prepare a new dish for your
dinner. Visit your local bookstore and look through the
cookbooks geared to the beginning cook. An excellent one
is Barbara Swain's *Cookery for 1 or 2*. Read through the

book, checking off the recipes that interest you. Make a checklist of the basic kitchen tools you will need as well as the ingredients. Buy them. And then try your first dish. You will probably discover early on that cooking can be both fun and easy. Within a few months you will have developed a repertoire of favorite dishes that you can prepare with little effort or time. And few things so impress a lady friend or wife as a tasty meal attractively prepared and served up by candlelight.

Dependency or interdependence is our choice to make. The Road of Dependency leads to emotional instability in our relationships with women. On the other hand, the Road of Interdependence leads to a different set of options: mutuality in our relationships with women, and the pride and security that come with the knowledge that we have those survival skills which will allow us to attend to our physical needs. Should we suddenly find ourself on our own or our wife or woman friend be stricken ill, we would be capable of taking care of ourselves.

THE BENEFITS OF CLEANING UP OUR ACT WITH WOMEN

1. **We gain female companionship.** We attract substantial women and elicit the best that female companionship has to offer. A female companion provides something special in a man's life that he can get nowhere else. Women as friends complement men in an unselfish, non-competitive way.

2. **We gain further access to the world of intuition and feeling.** Men also benefit from their relationships with women in the area of emotional health

and intuition. Women have long felt much freer to
express their feelings. They thus serve as useful
models for a more intuitive-based living. By in-
teracting with women, we men are better able to
balance the pragmatic, rational orientation we
adopted while growing up male.

3. **We gain an understanding and supportive
friend.** Having an understanding and supportive
woman friend is a godsend in times of need or can
add that special touch in an otherwise ordinary
day. A chat over the phone or a visit over lunch
with such a friend can favorably change your
mood for the rest of the day. Such an accepting
friendship can be enormously liberating because
with her you need not play any of the male roles.
You are free to be your true self.

4. **We improve as parents.** For those of us who
have chosen to father children, a final benefit is
that parenting reaches new levels of cooperation.
We better understand our wife's abilities and interests, and she ours. We communicate better. She
is attuned to our parenting abilities and interests
and does not buy into the "men are helpless"
stereotypes which exclude us from large areas of
our children's lives. And our children benefit
from a more loving and stable environment, in
which they will learn a model of intimacy and
cooperation that will sustain them the rest of their
lives.

GOING FACE TO FACE WITH A WOMAN

Without our dependency, fear, anger, and false images of Mother, we can come face to face with a woman. We can at last see what our life partner, who also happens to be a woman, is really like. Suddenly, we find ourselves noticing details about her that we never bothered to observe before.

EXERCISE NO. 3

Let's take an inventory of what your current awareness is when it comes to that most important woman in your life. First, read through the list below. Then go back and place a number 1, 2, or 3 in the space before each, indicating whether that item ranks at the top, in the middle, or at the bottom of your list in terms of its importance.

I am aware of:

_____ her hair

_____ her eyes

_____ her pet peeves

_____ her sexual turn-ons

_____ her idea of romance

_____ her frustrations at work

_____ her academic achievements

_____ her childhood roots

_____ her emotional pain

_____ her legs

_____ what she dreams

_____ her political opinions

_____ her professional ambitions

_____ how she moves

_____ her favorite gourmet dish

_____ her feelings toward her parents

_____ her breasts

_____ her clothes

_____ her biggest fears

_____ her sexual fantasies

_____ her ideas on marriage

_____ her successes at work

_____ her sports interests

_____ her favorite flower

_____ her feelings toward me

_____ her buttocks

_____ how she smells

_____ her favorite books

_____ her philosophy on life

_____ her interests and hobbies

_____ her looks

_____ her best friend

_____ other: _____

Now write down five items you listed under each category:

#1 Most Important	#2 Medium Important	#3 Least Important
_____	_____	_____
_____	_____	_____
_____	_____	_____

_____   _____   _____

_____   _____   _____

Look over your list above. How much do you really know about your life partner or woman friend as a person in her own right? How much has your attention been focused on her? How much on her image? Circle the ways you would like to get to know her better.

HOW CAN WE GET OUR WIVES BACK AS OUR FRIENDS?

I did not realize it at the time but when I married Karen I lost my best friend. She had become my wife.

Perhaps the greatest loss that long-term relationships suffer is that of friendship between the two partners. I learned this in my marriage with Karen when I realized that our friendship had faded. In due course, we discovered what had happened and managed to turn the situation around. But many couples are not that fortunate.

Soon after Karen and I first met, we had become the best of friends. I brought her home one evening to meet my roommates, one of whom she started dating, and introduced her to my girlfriend. When the four of us went out together for an evening, Karen and I always seemed to end up together, laughing and getting lost in lengthy discussions. Later I often found myself thinking of Karen and how happy we had made one another. Karen was the most joyful woman I had ever known. She brought out the best, most loving parts of me. Karen felt the same way about me. And so we eventually began what is today a sixteen-

year-old partnership. But something terrible happened to us
along the way. While we continued to be married, we
stopped being best friends.

Friendships fade for a variety of mostly poor reasons.
Ours was no exception. Caught up in the seriousness and
responsibilities of everyday living, we simply stopped
feeding our friendship. We starved it of lightheartedness,
spontaneity, silliness, sensuality, and, most of all, quality
time. While we were starving our friendship of its replen-
ishing nutrients, we were at the same time burdening it
with more demands and pressures, a lethal combination.

Could it be that two people living in the same house,
raising the same children, and sleeping in the same bed had
become strangers? Was it possible that two people who, not
long before could not get enough of each other's company,
were now frequently bored with each other? Yes, that was
exactly what had happened to us. Both Karen and I had
each lost our best friend.

When we discovered what had happened, both of us
became despondent. The void that had opened in our lives
seemed a black abyss that would not go away. Our friendship was nowhere to be found, not even in those precious
places where it had thrived for so many years. I remember
one cold evening in Colorado when, out of sheer frustration, we stayed up the entire night to see if, by pretending
to be "best friends," we could break through our barriers of
fear and hostility. That night Karen and I proceeded to
open up to each other about how our lives had really been.
Feelings that we had withheld from one another slowly
emerged and, with them, an appreciation of one another.
What had begun as a game became a beautiful awakening
of feelings long dormant. We discovered that being "best
friends" was and had always been a few moments of trust

away. But when we allowed fear and hostility to enter the relationship, those moments had seemed light-years away. Becoming friends again was not what it had been when we were 20 years old. But Karen and I did fall in love all over again as 35-year-old friends.

Through our simple little game of "Best Friends," Karen and I realized that our marriage was missing the basic friendship we had once enjoyed with one another. We could no longer talk to one another as friends for a variety of reasons. In this next exercise you are invited to consider how you might become a better friend with your own wife or lover.

EXERCISE NO. 4

Let's try to identify those areas in which you hold back from your partner. Check the appropriate responses:

I could be a better, more fun friend if I would only:

_____ let down and relax more around her
_____ let go and be more playful when I'm with her
_____ show her my romantic side
_____ be less serious around her sometimes
_____ stop being so cautious and guarded around her
_____ not be so easily offended
_____ be less controlling and follow her lead sometimes
_____ approach the situation more trustingly
_____ stop being so judgmental
_____ be less afraid of saying what I really feel

_____ have more confidence in myself

_____ stop making excuses such as "I'll be happy when . . ."

_____ stop postponing the pleasures of life

_____ stop trying to live up to some image

_____ get over my anger and forgive her

_____ stop worrying about what every little thing means

_____ get the rest I need

_____ eat well and exercise regularly, so that I will have more energy

Empathy is the ability to understand from the perspective of another person. Such understanding is power in the hands of those who wish to use the time and energy they spend in relationships making love, not wars.

The following exercises are to be used by male-female partners for the purpose of building understanding between the sexes. They have proven exciting catalysts for developing opportunities for new openness and appreciation between men and women. The purpose of these exercises is to generate the kind of personal information necessary for a full understanding of one another. There are no correct responses and no conclusions to reach. So do not pressure yourself to "perform" during these talks. Think of them as informal sharing between friends.

EXERCISE NO. 5

Set some time aside with your partner for a discussion on what it would be like to be the opposite sex. Before you dismiss this one, remember that *Tootsie*, one of the most popular films in recent years, took this as its central theme. You might begin by saying, "The things I could do as a man/woman that I cannot easily do now because I am a man/woman are:"

a) _____

b) _____

c) _____

EXERCISE NO. 6

Hold a discussion with your partner by answering the question: "The part of myself I find most difficult to share with someone of the opposite sex is _____." Remember that honesty in this area produces intimacy.

EXERCISE NO. 7

This exercise is great for getting unstuck when the two of you are hopelessly locked in a power struggle. Pretend to be your partner. Switch identities and roles for twenty minutes. "You be me and I'll be you" is a quick way to see how stubbornly we all hold on to our self-righteous positions. And it also allows us to go beyond those positions to new ones based on mutual understanding.

Each time Karen and I have included our two daughters, we have come away with a gem of new understanding

about their world. They become little directors, telling us
our roles and lines. This gives us an interesting perspective
on how the kids actually see us and how they feel about the
balance of power in our relationship.

EXERCISE NO. 8

The next time your wife or lover attends a meeting or an
event specifically oriented toward women, accompany her.
Focus your attention on your partner's feelings and actions
as a woman. See how the "other half" lives and interacts.

On several occasions I have accompanied my wife,
Karen, to meetings on women's business where I was the
only man present. Once I got over the feeling of being
literally the "odd man out," I learned a great deal about my
wife by watching her be a woman among women.

EXERCISE NO. 9

Interview your partner on what it was like growing up
female in her family. If she had a brother, how did she feel
being the other-sex sibling?

ADDING THE "LITTLE TOUCHES" TO YOUR RELATIONSHIP

"Why is it that a wife always works harder at making
the marriage go?" my friend Barbara once asked me. "Why
must I always be the one to think up clever, unique, and
'special' ways to keep the relationship fresh and exciting,

while my husband can't even remember to say, 'I love you'?"

Barbara went on. "Here's some advice for those men who are always insisting they can't figure out what women want. A woman does things for her man that she wishes he'd do for her. She says things to her man that she would love to hear him say to her."

The sad fact is that we men do not protect or promote our relationship "investments" with the same degree of care or interest that we do with our money investments. We usually wait for a crisis before we reevaluate what we are putting into our relationships. But by then many relationships are near bankruptcy.

Let us take an opportunity to assess how well we are protecting or promoting our relationship "investment" with our wife or woman friend. We all know the familiar pattern that most men follow in a relationship. They come out of the starting gate like a ball of fire—and then die in the homestretch. Mr. Wonderful turns into Mr. Dull.

Why, as the months and years go by, does the fire grow dimmer and dimmer? What causes us to stop adding those little touches or to remember them only on special occasions?

EXERCISE NO. 10

Stop for a moment and ask yourself, "What special things did I *used* to do for my wife or woman friend that I have since stopped doing?" Use the list below as a guide.

_____ buy her   _____ take her
flowers and   dancing
candy

_____ more foreplay before sex	_____ rate her "better than" other women
_____ use "pet" names	_____ sing her love songs
_____ whisper sweet nothings	_____ say, "I love you"
_____ take her out to dinner	_____ make love more often
_____ secretly surprise her	_____ take her out on the town
_____ give her back rubs	_____ pay her compliments
_____ be more creative at lovemaking	_____ "mini"-celebrations
_____ be more aggressive in pursuing her	_____ sacrifice for her
	_____ give her love gifts
	_____ other: _____

Let's try to figure out how these little touches faded from your relationships. Plug each item marked above into the following:

1. The reason I stopped _____ , or only do
   it on special occasions, is _____ .

2. The excuse I give myself and her for not doing
   _____anymore, or not doing it as much
   any longer, is _____ .

3. Check off whether this statement is true or false:
   I will trade my excuses for the love that will likely
   come back if I act more demonstrative.
   _____ true   _____ false

A MAN'S CREDO REGARDING WOMEN

- I will seek to succeed in adult-to-adult relationships by meeting women in their own right, not by
  chasing after "fantasy lovers" the way I did when I
  was a teenager. I am a grown man, comfortable
  with my maleness, and at ease in my relationships
  with my parents, my close male friends, and my
  work. Therefore, I am ready to meet women, face
  to face, and accept them as they are without trying
  to fit them into preconceived stereotypes.

- I will face the ways in which I depend in an unhealthy way on women, emotionally and for
  everyday survival, and make myself more self-
  sufficient. I will develop simple skills so that I
  can provide basic care for both myself and others.
  And I will learn emotional self-care, so that I can
  cope during those times when I am alone.

- I will differentiate between "Motherlove" and
  "Womanlove" in my relationships with women. I
  will stop expecting automatically that the purpose
  of women is to take care of my basic needs. I will
  commit myself to "Womanlove," which, like its
  counterpart "Manlove," is the love a woman freely
  chooses to give because she wants to, not because
  she feels she owes it to a man.

• I will trade in the "childish" mind-set I may secretly carry around for a whole, more complete
image of myself as a man. This does not mean that
I will kill off the "little boy" within me. Instead I
will give him spontaneous expression as an adult,
always remembering that grown men *can* be playful. Nor will I mistake the "childish" for the
"childlike" part in me.

As human beings, we all strive for fulfillment, wanting
the best that life has to offer. We try to balance that fine
line between accepting what we have and trying for
"more." But sometimes the line becomes blurred. We feel
torn in half, one side reprimanding us to "be ashamed for
not being content with what we have," while the other side
prods us to "have it all."

Could it be that both sides have something valuable to
tell us? We must accept what we have, respect our limits,
be all we can, do all we can do, and break through to new
frontiers of personal achievement.

One solution is to make the most of our existing relationships. We must decide to stop living complacently in
those relationships that are special to us. Instead we must
determine to bet on ourself and our relationships. And bet
to win, not to place or show.

🇫🇫🇫🇫🇫🇫🇫 Chapter EIGHT

Proud to Be a Man

Throughout this book, we have discussed "coming to terms" and applied this concept to our relationships with our parents, friends, and life partners. In this final chapter our emphasis will be on coming to terms with one's own self. This means we must accept the self that is us and take pride in who we really are. For some of us, this can only occur after we let go of a false male pride that we carry around, a superficial "macho" exterior that reflects little of our true nature. False pride is the last secret hiding place out of which we must come face to face with ourselves.

NO MORE HIDING BEHIND FALSE MALE PRIDE

False male pride means not allowing ourselves to be affected by our emotional needs and not letting anyone push us around. Males are told to "keep a stiff upper lip" and "never back down from a fight." But this pride is born of fear, a fear that our manhood is on the line.

There are two dangerous consequences of this kind of pride. First, it blocks us from an awareness of our true needs and feelings. We may be starved for affection, lonely, frightened, or in deep despair. But this limiting concept of manhood keeps us from admitting our feelings, either to ourselves or to others. The danger, then, is that our real needs go unrecognized and unmet.

Another consequence of false male pride is that it often turns into protective aggression. We defensively back ourselves and others into corners, closing off alternate channels of communication, understanding, and problem solving.

Pride that prevents us from meeting our needs or that leads to a life of continuous confrontation with others is a false pride. We want to nurture, instead, a form of male pride born of genuine self-esteem and confidence.

Genuine pride is a state of high self-purpose and esteem that arises out of the knowledge and acceptance of who and what we really are as men. Genuine pride inspires us to reach for the best in ourselves. It is born of courage, strength, persistence, patience, and honest self-acceptance.

To come to terms with themselves today, men need to stand proud, individually and collectively, without resorting to defensive "macho" pride.

PRIDE OR APOLOGIES FOR BEING A MAN?

Where do we stand on the issue of pride in being a man? Are we ashamed or proud to be a man? Is there something in our basic male nature that makes us ashamed? What about our maleness makes us proud?

Whatever our answer, isn't it time to give ourselves the appreciation that we deserve? Accepting ourselves means counting up the good in our lives and renewing our sense of genuine pride in ourselves as men.

So often we make the mistake of looking exclusively to others for recognition. At the end of every Alive and Male seminar, I ask each participant to take a moment to express his gratitude and appreciation toward himself. Each one takes his turn in front of the group. Some men cite themselves for something they have accomplished, perhaps that very day during the seminar. Others acknowledge their role as a son, father, husband, or friend. And still other men recognize qualities, such as patience, gentleness, and openness, that they are developing. The mood of the entire group becomes prideful. In a society which teaches men that their real value lies in achieving more, better, and faster, a man's genuine expression of love and regard for himself is a wonderfully moving experience.

LEARNING TO VALUE YOUR "SELF"

Men's secrets are out. Hopefully, we can begin to feel considerably less alone than before. Before, we may have had the tendency to deny ourselves the right to feel uncertain, fearful, weak, or hurt. We may have been more closely tied, psychologically and emotionally, to our fathers and mothers than we cared to admit. Perhaps we hid a strong desire for acceptance, support, and emotional openness with our male friends. Or, we may have used the workplace as a hiding place rather than a stage on which some of our greatest performances in life take place. Or, we may have been more dependent upon women for a sense of personal validity and acceptance than we cared to admit. And finally, we may have hidden behind a false "macho" pride.

The time has come for us not only to see that we men are all in this together but to *act* as brothers. We cannot progress further until we accept who and what we are, secrets and all. We may have long felt that we can do better. And we can. By focusing too long on what we perceived as our shortcomings and not enough on our merits, we men suffered the loss of precious self-esteem. If we feel good about ourselves, we can face whatever adversity comes along. What we value ourselves for and honestly feel about ourselves is every bit as important to our health as our daily diet of foods.

Can self-esteem be improved?

Of course! Those images we hold of ourselves are learned, not inherited. We all have an amazing capacity for flexibility and growth. Think of those friends and acquaintances who have come back even stronger after a bankruptcy, loss of a job, or severe illness. Sometimes self-esteem can be elevated merely by knowing that we are not alone in our problems—that we are not the only ones to feel such emotions.

How much are we "worth"?

If we are like most men, we will figure our "self-worth" by adding up all our material assets—our house, car, stocks, furniture, anything of value that can be sold. And this total would then be our "worth". Our sense of intrinsic self-worth is often intermingled with our material worth. They sometimes become one.

Each of us develops a unique way of thinking about our overall value to ourself, our family, our friends, our office mates, and the world in which we live. Nothing has a more powerful effect on our personality than our perception of our own sense of worth.

The value to us of a greater sense of self-approval cannot be measured. No amount of hard work, graduate education, money, power, social prestige, or love from others can ever substitute for a positive feeling about ourself.

Let us become the artist of our own lives, using the context of our daily living and interaction with others as the artistic medium out of which we will create our greatest masterpiece. This book sets forth a challenge for the coming months and years. New horizons for intimacy, friendship, success, and inner contentment lie before us. Through our participation in the exercises in these chapters, we have put together a manual that is truly unique.

What better guide to our future growth and development could we want? All that remains is for us to take ourself seriously. Nothing can provide a greater feeling of pride and accomplishment than living our life by our own script. As we watch it unfold, we will have every reason to hold our head high and be proud.

THE BENEFITS OF TAKING CHARGE

Our approach from the beginning has been to finish up the leftover business from our childhood, letting go of the old fears and images which no longer serve us. *We* are now in charge of our own life. Not our parents. Not our teachers. Not our boss. Not society. We are.

We have stopped seeing ourselves as victims, complaining about what the world has done to us. Instead of starting sentences with "I can't..." and "I have to...," we can

begin by saying, "I won't..." and "I choose to..." Feel
the difference as we say the words. We will certainly feel
more powerful and in charge if we say, "I want success"
instead of "I can't succeed." Once we accept that we and
we alone are responsible for our own lives and that virtually everything we do is ultimately a matter of personal
choice, then our options become virtually unlimited.

Let's look briefly at some of the benefits that flow to us
when we take charge of our own lives.

- We develop a greater sense of personal pride,
  knowing that we have achieved the best of which
  we are capable and taking assurance from the fact
  that we are our own man.

- We are more attuned to our needs and feelings and
  therefore work in concert with our minds and
  bodies. There is less psychological wear and tear
  on our nervous systems and significantly less conflict in our psyches.

- We feel more connected to the people who are important to us. We experience an increased capacity
  to give and receive love. We feel less loneliness.
  Our communications are more direct, conveying to
  others more precisely our needs and wants and
  hearing theirs.

- We become more involved in the affairs of our
  own life. We get to "live" in our own show, rather
  than rehearsing and acting out somebody else's
  script of what "the good life" should be. What we
  do becomes more pertinent to who we are, thus
  giving us the optimal success and enjoyment out of
  life.

- We derive more pleasure and have more fun, having regained the playful child in us. We are now ready to enjoy the "lighter" side of life.

- We experience clutter-free relationships with people, experiencing them in their own right without interference from past images. Our relationships become more enjoyable and less of a struggle.

- We break the destructive father-son cycle of the past. We are now free to make ourselves more available to our sons, both physically and psychologically, so that they will not become the next generation in search of a father. Our sons will see what it is *really* like to be a man through their one-on-one contact with us, their fathers. From us, they will gain a fundamental belief in themselves, a set of healthy expectations, and the self-confidence to choose wisely from the broadest range of options.

FULLY EXERCISING OUR FREEDOM OF CHOICE

Finally, let's review a list of nine freedoms that best ensure our happiness and well-being as men.

- I am free to feel and tend my emotions. I will not sidestep my feelings. Nor will I any longer ask women to take care of them for me.

- I am free of unhealthy ties to my father. I incorporate only the best my father had to give me, choosing to let go of any negative feelings I have from my past relationship with him.

- I am free to like and love my fellow men. I am not limited exclusively to female companions. My relationships with male friends are supportive, free of irrational fears and destructive competitiveness, emotionally intimate, and vitally refreshing.

- I am free to be interdependent with my fellow humans. I am not a slave to doctrines of self-reliance, choosing instead to accept help from others in my life when I need it. I am in control of my life enough to recognize that no man is an island entirely unto himself, including me.

- I am free of unhealthy ties to my mother. I take only the best my mother had to give me, choosing to let the past be.

- I am free to design my workstyle after my lifestyle. I use work as both a metaphor for what I am trying to accomplish in life and a positive source of self-development. I am not what I do. Rather, I do the work of that occupation.

- I am free of old myths which restrict my competence as an involved, loving father, a resourceful home manager, and an individual who can adequately care for his own basic needs. I am not helpless or dependent because I have made the development of these skills a top priority.

- I am free to share myself more openly with women instead of locking them out. I am willing to be vulnerable and intimate, and I expect the same from the women in my life. I relate to a woman as the person she is, not according to a set of distorted images and fantasies.

- And finally, I am free to feel proud of my manhood. I have no reason to apologize as a man. Nor do I have a license to push people around behind a false, inflated sense of male superiority. My pride is based on that which is good and beautiful in me as a man. I will use all that is in me as a man, and all that the great, peaceloving men of the ages have passed down, to make this world a better-safer place for future generations.

A Call for Reactions

Dr. Druck invites both men and women to contribute to his ongoing research on men. He asks the readers to send him their reactions to the book as well as anecdotes regarding memorable experiences with their fathers, mothers, children, wives, girlfriends, work, buddies, and brothers/sisters. Please state your age, schooling, employment, marital status, and any other biographical information that you wish. Anonymity is guaranteed.

Please send to:

Dr. Ken Druck
P.O. Box 3333 #160
Encinitas, CA 92024.

You may also write to this address for further information about speaking engagements and ALIVE AND MALE seminars taking place in your area.

About The Authors

DR. KEN DRUCK holds a doctorate in clinical psychology from the Fielding Institute, and maintains a private practice in San Diego. Dr. Druck lectures and offers his seminar, "Alive and Male," across the United States. His present research, in conjunction with the U.S. Department of State, deals with male psychology in the context of international negotiations.

JAMES C. SIMMONS is a freelance writer who has published two books and over two hundred magazine articles. He also has a doctorate in literature from the University of California at Berkeley.

SELF-HELP
from
BALLANTINE

By the year 2000, 2 out of 3 Americans could be illiterate.

It's true.

Today, 75 million adults...about one American in three, can't read adequately. And by the year 2000, U.S. News & World Report envisions an America with a literacy rate of only 30%.

Before that America comes to be, you can stop it...by joining the fight against illiteracy today.

Call the Coalition for Literacy at toll-free **1-800-228-8813** and volunteer.

**Volunteer
Against Illiteracy.
The only degree you need
is a degree of caring.**

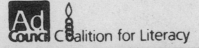

Ad Council   Coalition for Literacy   LV-2